Path to Inner Greatness

Unlocking Your
True Potential

Gina Parks

Chapter 1: Understanding Your Core Being

The Essence of Self Discovery

Self-discovery is a journey that begins with peeling back the layers of noise, expectation, and external influence to reveal the essence of who you truly are. At its core, it is not about becoming someone new but uncovering the authentic self that has always been there, waiting to be understood. This process requires a profound willingness to confront uncomfortable truths, embrace vulnerabilities, and challenge long-held assumptions about identity. The essence of self-discovery lies not in perfection but in authenticity, in the ability to stand unshaken in the face of one's truth.

Society often sets the framework for who we are supposed to be. From childhood, we are shaped by cultural norms, familial expectations, and social pressures, each of which crafts an image of how we should act, think, and even dream. Over time, this external molding can obscure the person you are at your core. Self-discovery begins when you consciously decide to strip away these imposed layers and examine which parts of you are genuine and which have been adopted to meet external approval. This is not an easy task—it demands courage to discard what no longer serves you and to question the beliefs you've carried for years. Yet, it is in this questioning that clarity emerges.

One of the most powerful ways to delve into self-discovery is through reflection. Reflection is not simply about recounting past events or experiences but about seeking meaning in them. Why do certain memories linger while others fade? What do your reactions to particular situations reveal about your inner world? By revisiting moments of joy, pain, success, and failure, you begin to discern patterns in your thoughts, emotions, and behaviors. These patterns act as signposts, guiding you toward a deeper understanding of your values, fears, and desires.

Central to self-discovery is the process of identifying values. Values act as the compass that directs your choices, relationships, and goals. They are the principles that resonate deeply within you, shaping how you perceive the world and your place in it. Yet, many people go through life without consciously acknowledging their core values, leading to a sense of disconnection and misalignment. To uncover these values, consider moments in your life when you felt most fulfilled or conversely, most conflicted. What was at stake during those times? What did you stand to gain or lose? Through these questions, you may begin to articulate the ideals that matter most to you.

Self-discovery also involves an exploration of beliefs. Beliefs, unlike values, are often formed unconsciously through upbringing, culture, and personal experiences. While some beliefs empower and uplift, others can act as barriers, limiting your potential and distorting your perception of reality. For instance, a belief that you are not good enough or that success is unattainable might hold you back from pursuing opportunities or taking risks. Examining these beliefs with a critical eye allows you to separate those that serve you from those that do not. In doing so, you create space for growth and transformation.

An often-overlooked aspect of self-discovery is the uncovering of hidden talents. Every individual possesses unique strengths and abilities, yet these can remain dormant when overshadowed by self-doubt or societal expectations. These talents may not always align with conventional definitions of success but hold immense value in shaping your sense of identity and purpose. Pay attention to the activities that bring you joy and the tasks that feel effortless yet fulfilling. These are often clues to your innate abilities. By nurturing these talents, you not only enrich your own life but also contribute something meaningful to the world around you.

The journey of self-discovery is deeply intertwined with self-awareness. To know oneself is to recognize not only what lies on the surface but also the intricate workings of the mind and heart. Self-awareness involves observing your thoughts without judgment, acknowledging your emotions without suppression, and understanding the motivations behind your actions. It is a state of mindfulness that allows you to live with intention rather than on autopilot. This awareness is not static; it evolves as you grow and adapt, offering new insights into your essence at every stage of life.

Barriers to self-discovery often come in the form of self-imposed limitations. These limitations are the mental constructs that convince you certain paths are out of reach or certain dreams are unattainable. They are born from fear—fear of failure, rejection, or the unknown—and they thrive in environments of doubt and complacency. Breaking through these barriers requires a shift in perspective. Instead of viewing challenges as obstacles, see them as opportunities for growth. Instead of fearing failure, embrace it as a stepping stone toward understanding and improvement. Each time you push beyond a perceived limitation, you expand your sense of what is possible and draw closer to your authentic self.

Self-discovery is not a destination but a continuous process. It is a journey marked by moments of clarity and confusion, triumph and struggle. What makes it worthwhile is the profound connection it fosters with oneself. It is in understanding who you are that you begin to live with greater purpose, meaning, and fulfillment. Through self-discovery, you gain the strength to navigate life's complexities with confidence and authenticity, knowing that you are grounded in the truth of your being.

Identifying Your Values and Beliefs

Values and beliefs form the foundation of who you are, guiding your decisions, shaping your relationships, and influencing how you navigate the world. They are the unseen forces that drive your behavior and determine your sense of purpose. Yet, many people go through life unaware of these internal frameworks, allowing external influences to dictate their choices. Identifying your values and beliefs is not merely an exercise in introspection—it is an act of empowerment. By uncovering these core truths, you gain clarity about what truly matters to you and begin to align your actions with your authentic self.

Values are the principles and standards that define what you hold as most important in life. They are deeply personal and often shaped by experiences, upbringing, and cultural context. While some values remain consistent throughout your life, others evolve as you grow and encounter new perspectives. For instance, the value of independence may have been instilled in you during childhood, but as you mature, you might find yourself prioritizing connection and community. The key to identifying your values is to look beyond societal expectations and ask yourself what truly resonates with your spirit. Consider the moments when you felt most alive or fulfilled—what were the underlying principles driving those experiences? These reflections offer valuable insights into what you deeply cherish.

Beliefs, on the other hand, are the convictions you hold about yourself, others, and the world. They are shaped by a combination of personal experiences, familial teachings, cultural narratives, and even the environments in which you have lived. Unlike values, beliefs can be either empowering or limiting. For example, believing in your ability to overcome challenges can propel you toward success, while believing that you are inherently inadequate can hold you back. The challenge lies in discerning which beliefs serve your growth and which hinder it. To do this, you must examine your thoughts critically and question their origins. Where did this belief come from? Is it based on fact or assumption? Does it align with your values? By engaging in this process, you begin to separate inherited beliefs from those you consciously choose to hold.

The interplay between values and beliefs is intricate and significant. Values often act as the foundation upon which beliefs are built, but beliefs can sometimes distort or obscure your values. For instance, if you value authenticity but hold a belief that being yourself will lead to rejection, you may inadvertently suppress your true nature. Conversely, when your beliefs align with your values, they create a sense of harmony and purpose. To achieve this alignment, it is essential to bring your values and beliefs into conscious awareness and evaluate how they interact.

One effective way to identify your values and beliefs is through self-reflection. Take time to analyze the decisions you've made, the relationships you've built, and the goals you've pursued. What patterns emerge? What do these patterns reveal about your priorities? Journaling can be a particularly useful tool in this process, as it allows you to explore your thoughts and feelings in a structured way. Another approach is to consider your reactions to specific situations. What makes you feel angry, proud, or deeply moved? These emotional responses often point to underlying values and beliefs.

Another powerful method is to examine your role models and the qualities you admire in them. Whether it's a parent, mentor, or historical figure, the traits you respect in others can provide clues to your own values. For instance, if you admire someone's resilience, it may indicate that perseverance is an important value for you. Similarly, observing the traits that frustrate or disappoint you in others can reveal values you prioritize but feel are missing in those interactions. These observations act as mirrors, reflecting the principles that matter most to you.

The process of identifying values and beliefs also involves confronting contradictions. It is not uncommon to discover that some of your beliefs conflict with your values, creating internal tension. For example, you may value kindness and compassion but hold a belief that vulnerability is a weakness, making it difficult to express empathy. Recognizing these contradictions is a crucial step toward resolving them. Once identified, you can work on reframing your beliefs to better align with your values. This often requires a willingness to challenge long-held assumptions and step outside your comfort zone.

As you uncover your values and beliefs, it's important to distinguish between those that are genuinely yours and those that have been imposed by others. Societal norms, familial expectations, and peer influence can all shape your internal frameworks in ways that may not align with your true self. For instance, you may have been taught to value material success, but upon reflection, you might realize that creativity and self-expression are more meaningful to you. Reclaiming your authentic values and beliefs involves shedding these external layers and embracing what feels right for you, regardless of external validation.

Identifying your values and beliefs is not a one-time exercise but an ongoing process. As you grow and evolve, so too will your understanding of what matters most. Life's experiences will continue to challenge and refine your perspectives, offering new opportunities for self-discovery. The more you engage with this process, the more equipped you become to live a life that is true to your essence. By aligning your actions with your values and embracing beliefs that empower you, you create a sense of purpose and fulfillment that is uniquely your own.

Uncovering Hidden Talents

Talents often lie dormant, hidden beneath layers of routine, doubt, and unexamined potential. Many people live their lives unaware of the unique abilities they possess, believing that talent is reserved for the exceptional few. But the truth is that everyone has gifts waiting to be discovered and nurtured. The process of uncovering hidden talents is not one of creation but revelation, a peeling back of the ordinary to expose the extraordinary that exists within. It requires curiosity, self-reflection, and the willingness to step into unfamiliar territory.

Hidden talents are not always obvious. They may not align with traditional skills, like painting or playing an instrument, nor do they need to fit into society's narrow definitions of what constitutes a "talent." Often, they manifest in subtle ways—an intuitive knack for understanding others, a natural ability to organize chaos, or an unspoken ease with solving complex problems. These abilities may seem ordinary to the person who possesses them, but to someone else, they are remarkable. The key to uncovering these talents lies in recognizing the activities or traits that feel inherently comfortable, almost effortless, yet yield extraordinary results.

One of the first steps in discovering hidden talents is revisiting your childhood. As children, we engage with the world with unfiltered curiosity and enthusiasm. We gravitate toward the things that bring us joy without worrying about their practicality or how they might be judged. Reflect on what you loved to do as a child. Did you spend hours drawing, building, writing stories, or organizing games with friends? These early inclinations often hold clues to your natural talents. While life's responsibilities may have pushed these interests to the background, they may still be present, waiting to be rekindled.

Feedback from others can also illuminate talents you might not recognize in yourself. Sometimes, what comes easily to you can seem so natural that you assume it's unremarkable. However, others may see these abilities in a different light, appreciating them in ways you don't fully comprehend. Pay attention to compliments or acknowledgments you've received over the years. Have people consistently praised your ability to listen, your problem-solving skills, or your creativity? These patterns of recognition often point to hidden strengths that you may have overlooked.

Experimentation is another essential component of uncovering hidden talents. Often, talents remain undiscovered because they simply haven't been given the opportunity to emerge. By stepping outside your comfort zone and trying new activities, you open the door to potential abilities you've never explored. This might mean taking a cooking class, joining a public speaking group, or volunteering for a leadership role. The goal is not immediate mastery but exploration. Through these experiences, you may stumble upon something that resonates deeply, sparking a sense of excitement and possibility.

It's also important to examine the moments when you lose track of time. These moments, often referred to as "flow states," occur when you are fully immersed in an activity, feeling both challenged and invigorated. Flow states are a powerful indicator of talent because they reveal what you are naturally drawn to. Think back to the last time you were so engaged in something that hours felt like minutes. What were you doing? These activities often align with your hidden strengths, offering a window into what you are uniquely equipped to excel at.

Fear and doubt often act as barriers to uncovering hidden talents. The fear of failure or judgment can prevent you from exploring new possibilities, while self-doubt can convince you that you lack the ability to succeed. Overcoming these barriers requires a shift in mindset. Instead of viewing talent as something you either have or don't have, see it as something that can be developed. Many talents start as small sparks that grow through practice, persistence, and a willingness to embrace imperfection. By giving yourself permission to try, fail, and try again, you create the conditions for your talents to emerge and flourish.

Hidden talents are not always glamorous or outwardly impressive, but their impact can be profound. A talent for connecting with others on a deep level can transform relationships and foster empathy. A knack for simplifying complex ideas can make you an invaluable teacher or communicator. These strengths may not garner public acclaim, but they hold immense value in shaping your identity and enriching the lives of those around you. Recognizing and embracing these abilities allows you to contribute to the world in ways that feel authentic and meaningful.

The process of uncovering hidden talents is deeply personal, but it is also dynamic. As you grow and evolve, new talents may emerge, while others may take on different forms. The journey is not about reaching a final destination but about remaining open to discovery and change. By continually exploring your interests, seeking feedback, and confronting your fears, you create a life that is in tune with your unique potential.

Uncovering your hidden talents is an act of self-empowerment. It allows you to step into your fullest expression, embracing not only what you know about yourself but also the possibilities you have yet to uncover. These talents, once brought to light, can enrich your life in ways you never imagined, offering new avenues for purpose, fulfillment, and contribution. The journey is as much about curiosity as it is about courage—the courage to believe that within you lies untapped greatness, waiting to be revealed.

The Power of Self Awareness

Self-awareness is the foundation upon which personal growth and meaningful connections are built. It is the ability to see yourself clearly, to understand your emotions, thoughts, and behaviors, and to recognize how they influence your decisions and relationships. Unlike fleeting moments of introspection, self-awareness is a continuous practice, an ongoing dialogue with yourself that fosters a deeper understanding of who you are and how you interact with the world. Its power lies in its ability to bring clarity to the complexities of life, enabling you to make choices that align with your values and aspirations.

At its core, self-awareness is about observation without judgment. It is the art of stepping back and examining your internal world with curiosity rather than criticism. For many, this can be a challenging task. The mind is often clouded by biases, assumptions, and ingrained patterns of thinking that distort reality. Yet, with consistent effort, these mental fogs can be cleared, revealing a more accurate and honest picture of yourself. This honesty is not about highlighting flaws but about embracing the entirety of who you are—the strengths, the weaknesses, the contradictions, and the potential. By doing so, you create a foundation of authenticity that allows you to navigate life with confidence and clarity.

One of the most significant benefits of self-awareness is its impact on emotional intelligence. Emotions are powerful forces that influence your thoughts, actions, and interactions with others. Without awareness, they can control you, leading to impulsive decisions or misunderstandings. However, when you develop the ability to recognize and name your emotions as they arise, you gain the power to respond rather than react.

For example, noticing that you feel frustrated during a conversation allows you to pause and reflect before speaking, preventing an emotional outburst that could damage the relationship. This level of emotional regulation not only enhances your own well-being but also fosters deeper and more meaningful connections with others.

Self-awareness also plays a crucial role in uncovering the patterns that shape your life. Every individual operates within a web of habits, beliefs, and assumptions that guide their behavior. Some of these patterns are constructive, while others may be limiting or even harmful. For instance, you might notice a recurring tendency to procrastinate when faced with challenging tasks or to avoid confrontation in difficult situations. By bringing these patterns to light, self-awareness gives you the opportunity to question their origins and evaluate whether they serve your goals. This process of reflection creates space for growth, allowing you to replace unhelpful habits with ones that align more closely with your values and aspirations.

The relationship between self-awareness and decision-making cannot be overstated. Every choice you make is filtered through your perception of yourself and the world around you. When that perception is clouded by a lack of self-awareness, your decisions may be driven by fear, insecurity, or external pressures rather than your true desires. Conversely, when you are deeply attuned to your values, priorities, and emotions, you can make choices that feel intentional and authentic. For example, instead of pursuing a career path because it is expected of you, self-awareness might reveal a passion or interest that aligns more closely with your sense of purpose. This alignment creates a sense of fulfillment that goes beyond external achievements, grounding you in a life that feels genuinely meaningful.

Developing self-awareness is not a passive process; it requires deliberate effort and practice. One of the most effective tools for cultivating it is mindfulness, the practice of paying attention to the present moment without judgment. By observing your thoughts, feelings, and physical sensations as they arise, you begin to notice patterns and triggers that might otherwise go unnoticed. For instance, you might become aware of the tightness in your chest when you feel anxious or the surge of energy that accompanies excitement. Over time, this heightened awareness allows you to respond to situations with greater clarity and intention.

Another powerful method for enhancing self-awareness is seeking feedback from others. While introspection is invaluable, it has its limitations. You are inherently biased in how you perceive yourself, and certain blind spots may remain hidden without external input. Trusted friends, family members, or mentors can provide insights into how your actions and demeanor are perceived, offering a new perspective on your strengths and areas for growth. Receiving feedback requires humility and openness, but it is one of the most effective ways to deepen your understanding of yourself.

The journey toward self-awareness is not always comfortable. It often requires confronting aspects of yourself that you might prefer to ignore, such as fears, insecurities, or past mistakes. However, it is precisely in this discomfort that the greatest growth occurs. By facing these truths with courage and compassion, you free yourself from their hold, allowing you to move forward with a sense of liberation and possibility. This process is not about achieving perfection but about embracing progress, recognizing that self-awareness is a lifelong journey rather than a destination.

The ripple effects of self-awareness extend far beyond the individual. When you understand yourself, you are better equipped to understand others. Empathy, the ability to put yourself in someone else's shoes, is rooted in self-awareness. By recognizing your own emotions and experiences, you gain the capacity to appreciate the perspectives of others, even when they differ from your own. This empathy fosters stronger relationships, reduces conflict, and creates a sense of connection that enriches both personal and professional interactions.

Breaking Through Self Imposed Limitations

Self-imposed limitations are invisible walls we construct around ourselves, often without realizing it. They are the mental barriers that whisper, "You can't," even before you try. These limitations, rooted in fear, doubt, and past experiences, can feel so real that they shape the choices we make and the paths we follow. Yet, they are not as permanent as they seem. Breaking through them begins with identifying their presence, understanding their origins, and challenging their validity. It's a process that requires courage, but the rewards are transformative, unlocking a world of potential and possibility.

The origins of self-imposed limitations are often subtle, woven into the fabric of our lives by early experiences, social conditioning, and internalized expectations. A single moment, like being ridiculed for a mistake as a child, can plant the seed of a belief that you're not good enough. Over time, that belief takes root, shaping how you see yourself. Similarly, societal messages about what is "acceptable" or "achievable" can create narrow definitions of success, leading you to dismiss dreams that fall outside those boundaries. These limitations are often reinforced by repetition. The more you tell yourself you can't do something, the stronger that belief becomes, turning into a self-fulfilling prophecy.

Recognizing these limitations is the first step toward breaking free from them. This requires honest self-reflection and a willingness to confront uncomfortable truths. Pay attention to the stories you tell yourself about who you are and what you're capable of. Do you often think, "I'm not smart enough," or "I'll never be able to do that"? These thoughts are clues, pointing to the areas where self-imposed barriers may be holding you back. It's important to approach this process with compassion rather than judgment. These limitations are not flaws; they are simply beliefs that have outlived their usefulness.

Fear is one of the most common drivers of self-imposed limitations. Fear of failure, fear of rejection, fear of the unknown—all of these can keep you confined within a narrow comfort zone. While the comfort zone feels safe, it is also restrictive, preventing growth and exploration. To break free, you must confront these fears head-on. This doesn't mean eliminating fear altogether, as fear is a natural human emotion. Instead, it means learning to move forward in spite of it. Each time you face a fear and take action anyway, you weaken its grip on you, proving to yourself that you are stronger than you realized.

Negative self-talk is another powerful force behind self-imposed limitations. The inner critic, that voice in your mind that constantly points out your flaws and shortcomings, can be relentless. It's important to recognize that this voice is not an accurate reflection of reality. Often, it is simply an echo of past criticisms or insecurities. To silence the inner critic, start by questioning its validity. Is there evidence to support what it's saying, or is it based on assumptions? Replace negative self-talk with affirmations that reinforce your strengths and potential. Over time, this shift in mindset can help dismantle the barriers you've built.

Another way to break through self-imposed limitations is by re-framing failure. Many people avoid taking risks because they equate failure with inadequacy. However, failure is not the opposite of success—it is a stepping stone toward it. Every misstep, mistake, or setback provides valuable lessons that contribute to growth. Rather than viewing failure as an endpoint, see it as part of the process. Celebrate the courage it took to try, and use the experience to refine your approach. When failure is no longer something to fear, you open yourself up to opportunities you might otherwise have avoided.

Taking small, deliberate steps outside your comfort zone can also help dismantle self-imposed limitations. You don't need to make drastic changes overnight; even small actions can create momentum. Each time you push past a boundary, no matter how minor, you expand your sense of what is possible. For instance, if you believe you're not a good public speaker, start by speaking up in a small group. As you gain confidence, you can take on larger challenges, like giving a presentation. With each step, the limitations that once seemed insurmountable begin to fade.

Support from others can be invaluable in this journey. Friends, mentors, or even professional coaches can offer encouragement and perspective, helping you see possibilities you might have overlooked. Sometimes, an outside perspective is all it takes to challenge a deeply ingrained belief. Surround yourself with people who believe in you and who push you to strive for more. Their confidence in your abilities can be contagious, inspiring you to take risks and challenge your own doubts.

Breaking through self-imposed limitations requires persistence and resilience. There will be moments when progress feels slow or when old doubts resurface. During these times, it's important to remind yourself of the progress you've already made and the reasons why you started this journey. Reflect on the moments when you've overcome challenges in the past—they are proof of your strength and capability. Each breakthrough, no matter how small, is a victory that brings you closer to your fullest potential.

The process of overcoming self-imposed limitations is not just about achieving specific goals; it's about reclaiming your agency and redefining what is possible for you. It's about realizing that the barriers you thought were unbreakable were, in fact, of your own making—and therefore within your power to dismantle. As you move beyond these limitations, you discover not only new opportunities but also a deeper sense of self-worth and confidence. You come to understand that your potential is not fixed but limitless, shaped only by the boundaries you choose to accept or reject.

Chapter 2: Mindset Transformation

From Fixed to Growth Mindset

A mindset is a lens through which you view the world, shaping how you interpret challenges, respond to setbacks, and pursue opportunities. At the heart of personal development lies the distinction between a fixed mindset and a growth mindset. The former is anchored in the belief that traits such as intelligence, talent, and abilities are static—unchangeable from birth. The latter, in contrast, embraces the idea that these qualities can be cultivated through effort, learning, and perseverance. Transitioning from a fixed to a growth mindset is not just about adopting a new perspective; it's about transforming how you engage with life's experiences and unlocking your potential.

A fixed mindset often develops subtly, influenced by messages internalized from early experiences. Perhaps as a child, you were praised for being "smart" or "talented," setting the expectation that your worth was tied to innate qualities. While these compliments might have felt rewarding, they inadvertently created a fear of failure. If success is rooted in unchangeable traits, then failure becomes a threat to your identity. This mindset can lead to avoiding challenges, resisting effort, and shying away from opportunities that might expose your vulnerabilities. A fixed mindset thrives on the comfort of what is already known and mastered, but in doing so, it stifles growth and limits achievement.

A growth mindset, on the other hand, reframes challenges as opportunities for learning and development. It recognizes that effort is not a sign of weakness but a pathway to improvement. Those with a growth mindset view failure not as a reflection of their abilities but as a natural part of the learning process. They understand that skills and intelligence are not fixed assets but dynamic qualities that can be expanded through dedication and practice. This perspective fosters resilience, curiosity, and a willingness to take risks—all essential ingredients for personal and professional success.

The shift from a fixed to a growth mindset begins with awareness. Recognizing the limiting beliefs and thought patterns associated with a fixed mindset is the first step toward change. Pay attention to the language you use, both internally and externally. Do you often think or say things like, "I'm just not good at this," or "I'll never be able to do that"? These statements reflect a belief in static abilities and can be replaced with growth-oriented alternatives such as, "I'm not good at this yet," or "I can improve with practice." The simple act of modifying your language can have a profound impact on how you approach challenges and perceive your potential.

Effort plays a central role in cultivating a growth mindset. In a fixed mindset, effort is often seen as futile—if you have to try hard, it must mean you're not naturally capable. In a growth mindset, effort is celebrated as the mechanism through which growth occurs. Consider the process of learning a new skill, such as playing a musical instrument. Progress may be slow and frustrating at first, but with consistent practice, improvement becomes inevitable. Each stumble is a step toward mastery. Embracing effort as a necessary and valuable part of growth shifts your focus from immediate results to long-term development.

Failure, while often feared, is an essential component of the growth mindset. It provides valuable feedback, highlighting areas for improvement and revealing strategies that may not be effective. Rather than avoiding failure, those with a growth mindset seek to learn from it. This doesn't mean failure is easy or enjoyable, but it is seen as a temporary setback rather than a permanent roadblock. Each failure carries within it the seeds of growth, offering an opportunity to refine your approach and strengthen your resolve. By reframing failure as a teacher rather than an enemy, you build resilience and a willingness to push beyond your comfort zone.

The influence of others can also shape your mindset. Surrounding yourself with individuals who embody a growth-oriented perspective can inspire and motivate you to adopt similar attitudes. These individuals tend to focus on progress rather than perfection, celebrating effort and persistence over innate ability. Their encouragement and support can help reinforce your belief in your capacity for growth. Conversely, environments that emphasize fixed traits or judge failure harshly can reinforce limiting beliefs. Being mindful of the people and messages you engage with can play a significant role in fostering a growth mindset.

One of the most powerful tools for reinforcing a growth mindset is adopting a love for learning. Curiosity fuels exploration, and exploration fuels growth. When you approach life with a sense of wonder and a desire to understand more, you naturally gravitate toward challenges and opportunities for development. This mindset allows you to see setbacks not as obstacles but as puzzles to solve, enriching your journey rather than detracting from it. The more you cultivate this love for learning, the more resilient and adaptable you become, prepared to face the ever-changing demands of life.

The process of transitioning from a fixed to a growth mindset is not linear. Old patterns of thought may resurface, and moments of doubt are inevitable. However, each small step toward embracing growth builds momentum, creating a positive cycle of effort, learning, and achievement. Over time, the shift becomes more natural, and the fixed mindset loses its hold. With practice, you begin to see challenges as opportunities, failure as feedback, and effort as the bridge to success.

A growth mindset is more than just a belief in your ability to improve; it is a way of engaging with the world that fosters resilience, creativity, and fulfillment. It empowers you to take ownership of your development, to embrace the unknown, and to persevere in the face of adversity. By shifting your perspective from fixed limitations to boundless possibilities, you unlock the potential within yourself and open the door to a life of continuous growth and discovery.

Rewiring Negative Thought Patterns

Negative thought patterns can feel like an endless loop, replaying doubts, fears, and criticisms that shape how you see yourself and the world. These patterns often form gradually, built from experiences, beliefs, and interpretations that have solidified over time. They can distort reality, undermine confidence, and limit your ability to achieve your goals. Rewiring these patterns is not simply about replacing one thought with another; it's about reprogramming the way your mind processes and responds to challenges, setbacks, and daily life. This transformation requires awareness, intention, and persistence, but the result is a profound shift toward clarity, resilience, and self-empowerment.

Negative thought patterns often begin in subtle ways, triggered by experiences that carry emotional weight. A single critical comment, a perceived failure, or an unresolved fear can plant the seed of self-doubt. Over time, this doubt can grow, reinforced by similar experiences or the way you interpret them. Perhaps you've tried something and failed, leading to the belief that you're incapable. This belief becomes a lens through which you view future attempts, making each setback feel inevitable and confirming the narrative you've constructed. These patterns are self-perpetuating, as the mind tends to seek evidence that aligns with its existing beliefs while dismissing anything that contradicts them.

Recognizing these patterns is the first and most crucial step. You cannot rewire what you do not see. Pay attention to your inner dialogue, especially during moments of stress, failure, or uncertainty. Do you find yourself using absolutes, like "I always mess things up" or "Nothing ever works out for me"? These statements are red flags, signaling a fixed and overly negative perception of your abilities or circumstances. Notice the specific triggers and recurring themes in your thoughts. Awareness is not about judgment; it's about observing your mental habits with curiosity and detachment, creating space for change.

Once you've identified negative thought patterns, it's important to challenge their validity. These thoughts often feel true because they are deeply ingrained, but that does not mean they are accurate. Consider the evidence supporting these beliefs. Are they based on facts or assumptions? For example, if you believe you're not good at something because of one failed attempt, ask yourself whether one isolated incident truly defines your capabilities. Look for counterexamples—times when you succeeded or demonstrated resilience in similar situations. By questioning the foundations of your negative thoughts, you begin to weaken their hold and open the door to alternative perspectives.

Reframing is a powerful tool for rewiring negative thought patterns. This involves shifting your perspective to see situations in a more balanced and constructive light. It's not about ignoring challenges or pretending everything is perfect but about finding a more helpful way to interpret events. For instance, instead of viewing a mistake as proof of failure, you might see it as an opportunity to learn and grow. Instead of assuming someone's criticism was meant to hurt you, consider whether it might have been an attempt to offer guidance. Reframing allows you to replace self-defeating narratives with ones that empower and motivate you.

The language you use, both in your mind and aloud, plays a significant role in shaping your thought patterns. Negative language reinforces negative thinking, while positive or neutral language creates opportunities for growth. Pay attention to phrases like "I can't," "I'm not good enough," or "This is impossible." Replace them with more constructive alternatives, such as "I'll try," "I'm learning," or "This is challenging, but I can handle it." These subtle shifts in language signal to your brain that change is possible, gradually rewiring the way you respond to difficulties.

Mindfulness is another essential practice in breaking free from negative thought patterns. The mind often operates on autopilot, replaying the same thoughts without conscious awareness. Mindfulness trains you to observe your thoughts as they arise, creating a gap between the thought and your reaction to it. When a negative thought appears, instead of immediately accepting it as truth, you can acknowledge it and then let it pass without attaching to it. Over time, this practice weakens the automatic grip of negative patterns, allowing you to respond with greater awareness and intention.

It's also important to cultivate self-compassion throughout this process. Negative thought patterns often thrive on harsh self-criticism, creating a cycle of shame and defeat. Treating yourself with kindness and understanding disrupts this cycle, reminding you that imperfection is part of being human. When you catch yourself falling into negative thinking, resist the urge to berate yourself. Instead, acknowledge the thought, remind yourself that it's okay to struggle, and gently guide your mind toward a more constructive perspective. Self-compassion provides the emotional safety needed to explore and rewire deeply rooted patterns.

Building positive habits can help reinforce the rewiring process. Engaging in activities that boost your mood, such as exercising, journaling, or spending time with supportive people, creates a mental environment that is less conducive to negativity. Additionally, practicing gratitude can shift your focus from what's wrong to what's going well in your life. Writing down a few things you're grateful for each day trains your mind to notice and appreciate the positive, gradually rebalancing your mental outlook.

Rewiring negative thought patterns is not an overnight transformation but a gradual process of creating new neural pathways. Each time you challenge a negative thought, reframe a situation, or respond with self-compassion, you strengthen these new pathways, making them more automatic over time. There will be setbacks, but these are part of the journey. What matters is your commitment to the process and your belief in your ability to change.

The freedom that comes from breaking free of negative thought patterns is profound. It allows you to see yourself and the world with greater clarity, to approach challenges with confidence, and to live a life that feels aligned with your values and aspirations. By rewiring the way you think, you reclaim control over your mind, transforming it from a source of limitation into one of empowerment and possibility.

The Psychology of Success

Success is often perceived as the outcome of external circumstances: a fortunate break, an advantageous opportunity, or sheer talent. However, beneath these surface-level factors lies a deeper, more powerful force—the psychology that shapes how people think, act, and persevere in the pursuit of their goals. The psychology of success is not a fixed trait but a dynamic interplay of attitudes, beliefs, and behaviors that can be cultivated and strengthened over time. It governs how individuals respond to challenges, maintain focus, and push forward despite setbacks. Understanding and harnessing this psychology transforms success from a distant aspiration into a tangible and achievable reality.

The foundation of success begins with belief—belief in one's abilities, potential, and worthiness to achieve. This self-belief, often referred to as self-efficacy, is not simply confidence but a deep-seated conviction that you can influence the outcomes of your life through effort and determination. Without this belief, even the most capable individuals can falter, held back by doubts that undermine their resolve. Self-efficacy develops not from grand accomplishments but from small victories that build a sense of competence and control. Each challenge overcome and each milestone reached strengthens this inner certainty, creating a cycle of confidence and action that propels success.

A clear vision is another cornerstone of success. Those who achieve remarkable things often have a precise understanding of what they are working toward. This vision acts as both a compass and a motivator, providing direction and purpose. It narrows the focus, helping to filter out distractions and align efforts with meaningful goals. A successful vision, however, is not merely about ambition; it is also rooted in authenticity. When your goals resonate with your values and passions, the pursuit becomes deeply fulfilling, infusing the journey with energy and resilience. This alignment between vision and purpose unlocks a wellspring of motivation that sustains effort, even in the face of adversity.

The ability to embrace failure is a defining characteristic of those who succeed. Failure is often stigmatized, seen as a sign of inadequacy or a reason to abandon one's aspirations. Yet, in reality, failure is an inevitable and essential part of the journey. It provides the feedback necessary for growth, revealing what works and what doesn't, and offering opportunities to refine strategies and skills. Those with a success-oriented mindset view failure not as an endpoint but as a stepping stone. They approach setbacks with curiosity rather than despair, asking, "What can I learn from this?" This resilience transforms failure from a source of fear into a tool for progress.

An equally critical factor in the psychology of success is persistence. Talent and opportunity may open doors, but it is persistence that keeps them open. This tenacity is not about blindly pushing forward but about maintaining focus and effort over the long term, even when progress seems slow or obstacles appear insurmountable. Persistence is fueled by a combination of grit and adaptability—the determination to stay committed to your goals while remaining flexible enough to adjust your approach as circumstances change. This balance allows you to persevere without becoming stuck in ineffective patterns, ensuring that effort translates into meaningful results.

The role of mindset in success cannot be overstated. A fixed mindset, which perceives abilities and intelligence as static, can create a fear of challenges and a reluctance to take risks. In contrast, a growth mindset—one that sees abilities as malleable and capable of development through effort—fosters a willingness to embrace challenges and persist through difficulties. This mindset shift transforms obstacles into opportunities for learning and growth, creating a psychological environment in which success becomes not just possible but inevitable. Cultivating a growth mindset involves reframing how you view effort, setbacks, and feedback, recognizing them as integral components of the journey.

Success is also deeply influenced by emotional regulation. The ability to manage emotions, particularly under pressure, can mean the difference between giving up and pushing forward. Stress, frustration, and self-doubt are natural responses to challenges, but if left unchecked, they can derail progress. Those who succeed practice emotional resilience, developing strategies to stay calm, focused, and optimistic even in difficult circumstances. This might involve mindfulness techniques, reframing negative thoughts, or seeking support from others. By maintaining emotional equilibrium, you create the mental clarity needed to navigate complexities and make sound decisions.

Another key element in the psychology of success is the ability to take action. Many people have dreams and aspirations but become paralyzed by overthinking, fear of failure, or a desire for perfection. Success-oriented individuals understand that progress is made through doing, even when conditions are less than ideal. They prioritize action over hesitation, recognizing that each step forward, no matter how small, brings them closer to their goals. This proactive approach creates momentum, breaking through inertia and building confidence with each accomplishment. Action, even in its simplest form, transforms ideas into reality.

The environment you cultivate also plays a significant role in shaping your psychology for success. Surrounding yourself with supportive and inspiring individuals creates a network of encouragement and accountability. These relationships provide perspective, challenge you to grow, and celebrate your achievements. Conversely, environments filled with negativity or complacency can reinforce limiting beliefs and hinder progress. Being intentional about the people, habits, and influences you allow into your life creates a fertile ground for success to thrive.

Finally, gratitude serves as a powerful psychological tool in the pursuit of success. While ambition drives you forward, gratitude keeps you grounded, reminding you of the progress you've made and the resources you already possess. This balance prevents burnout, fostering a sense of contentment and perspective that sustains motivation. Gratitude shifts focus from what is lacking to what is present, creating a mindset of abundance that attracts further opportunities and growth.

The psychology of success is not a secret formula or a set of rigid rules. It is a dynamic interplay of beliefs, attitudes, and actions that work together to create momentum and achievement. By cultivating self-belief, maintaining a clear and authentic vision, embracing failure, and persisting through challenges, you align yourself with the principles that drive success. These psychological foundations are not reserved for a select few—they are accessible to anyone willing to cultivate them. Success begins and grows in the mind, and by mastering its psychology, you unlock the potential to achieve extraordinary things.

.

Chapter 3: Building Mental Resilience

Embracing Change and Uncertainty

Change and uncertainty are inevitable forces that weave through the fabric of life. They arrive unannounced, disrupting routines, challenging expectations, and often stirring feelings of discomfort or fear. Yet, they are also catalysts for growth, innovation, and transformation. The ability to embrace change and navigate uncertainty is not a matter of suppressing these emotions but of learning to coexist with them, to see opportunity within the unfamiliar, and to adapt with resilience and creativity. It is a mindset shift that turns what might feel like chaos into a stepping stone toward something greater.

Resistance to change is deeply rooted in human psychology. The brain is wired to favor predictability and routine, as these provide a sense of safety and control. When faced with the unknown, the mind often conjures worst-case scenarios or clings to familiar patterns, even when they no longer serve a purpose. This resistance can manifest as procrastination, denial, or an overwhelming need for certainty. However, clinging to what is comfortable may lead to stagnation, limiting the opportunities that come with stepping into the unknown. Recognizing this resistance as a natural response, rather than a roadblock, is the first step toward embracing change.

One of the most significant barriers to accepting change is fear—fear of failure, fear of making the wrong decision, or fear of losing what is familiar. These fears often stem from a desire to control outcomes, to ensure that every step forward is both precise and predictable. Yet life rarely unfolds in neat, linear progressions. Uncertainty is a constant companion, and attempting to eliminate it entirely is both futile and exhausting. Instead, the focus must shift to managing fear and uncertainty, acknowledging their presence without allowing them to dictate actions. This requires cultivating a sense of trust—not in the outcome, but in your ability to adapt and respond, regardless of what lies ahead.

Adaptability is a critical skill in navigating change. It is the capacity to remain flexible, to adjust your approach as circumstances evolve, and to find opportunity in disruption. Take, for example, those who have thrived in times of upheaval. Entrepreneurs who pivot their business models in response to shifting markets, individuals who reinvent their careers after unexpected layoffs, or communities that come together to rebuild after natural disasters—all demonstrate the power of adaptability. It is not about having all the answers but about being willing to explore new paths, to experiment, and to learn along the way.

Perspective plays a significant role in how change and uncertainty are experienced. The way a situation is framed can influence whether it is seen as a threat or an opportunity. For instance, losing a job may initially feel like a devastating setback, but it can also be reframed as a chance to pursue a more fulfilling career or develop new skills. Similarly, moving to a new city might evoke anxiety about leaving behind the familiar, yet it also offers the possibility of new connections and experiences. Shifting perspective does not deny the challenges of change but allows for a fuller exploration of its potential benefits.

Another key to embracing change is focusing on what can be controlled. While the external world is often unpredictable, your actions, attitudes, and choices remain within your sphere of influence. This sense of agency provides a foundation of stability amid uncertainty. It might involve setting small, achievable goals, maintaining routines that ground you, or taking deliberate steps toward a larger vision. These actions create momentum, fostering confidence and a sense of progress even when the broader picture remains unclear.

Resilience is built through the willingness to face discomfort and uncertainty head-on. Growth often occurs at the edges of your comfort zone, where the familiar gives way to the unknown. Each time you step into that space, you expand your capacity to handle challenges and adapt to change. Consider the metaphor of a muscle growing stronger through resistance. Just as physical strength is developed by pushing against weight, emotional and mental resilience is cultivated by leaning into difficulty rather than avoiding it. Each experience of navigating change becomes a lesson, adding to your toolkit for future challenges.

The role of curiosity in embracing change should not be overlooked. Approaching the unknown with a sense of wonder rather than dread transforms it into an adventure rather than a threat. Curiosity fuels exploration, encouraging you to ask questions, seek understanding, and remain open to new possibilities. It shifts the focus from fearing what might go wrong to discovering what might go right. This mindset fosters creativity and innovation, allowing you to see solutions and opportunities that might otherwise remain hidden.

Support from others can make a significant difference in how change and uncertainty are experienced. Sharing fears, seeking advice, or simply being in the presence of those who believe in your ability to adapt can provide reassurance and perspective. These connections remind you that you are not alone, that others have faced similar challenges and emerged stronger. At the same time, offering support to others creates a sense of reciprocity and purpose, reinforcing your own resilience while contributing to the well-being of those around you.

Embracing change does not mean eliminating all fear or uncertainty but learning to move forward despite them. It is about developing the confidence to take the first step, even when the path ahead is unclear, and trusting that clarity will come with action. It is about finding stability not in unchanging circumstances but in your own ability to adapt and persevere. Change is not a disruption to life—it is life. By leaning into it, you open yourself to growth, transformation, and the infinite possibilities that lie beyond the boundaries of the known.

Developing Emotional Intelligence

Emotional intelligence is the quiet force that shapes how we understand and navigate the complexities of human interaction. It governs how we perceive, manage, and respond to our own emotions and the emotions of others. Unlike cognitive intelligence, which is measured through academic achievements or problem-solving abilities, emotional intelligence is rooted in the subtleties of awareness and connection. It influences everything from personal relationships to professional success, serving as the foundation for empathy, resilience, and effective communication. While some individuals seem naturally attuned to their emotions and those of others, emotional intelligence is not an inherent trait—it is a skill that can be developed and refined with deliberate practice.

The first step in developing emotional intelligence is cultivating self-awareness. This involves recognizing and understanding your emotions as they arise, rather than allowing them to operate in the background. Too often, people react to situations without fully grasping the emotions driving their behavior. For example, a sharp comment in a meeting might stem not from anger at a colleague but from underlying stress or insecurity. Identifying these emotional triggers requires slowing down and observing your internal state with curiosity and without judgment. Journaling, mindfulness practices, or simply taking a moment to reflect during emotionally charged situations can help you build this awareness. Over time, you'll begin to notice patterns in your emotions and the circumstances that elicit them, providing valuable insight into your emotional landscape.

Once you've developed self-awareness, the next challenge is learning to manage your emotions effectively. Emotional regulation does not mean suppressing or ignoring your feelings but finding healthy ways to express and channel them. Anger, for instance, can be a destructive force when left unchecked, but it can also serve as a motivator for addressing injustices or advocating for change. Similarly, sadness may feel overwhelming, yet it can foster introspection and deeper understanding if given the space to be processed. The key is to create a pause between emotion and action, allowing yourself to choose a response that aligns with your values and goals. Techniques such as deep breathing, counting to ten, or reframing your perspective can help you regain control in the heat of the moment.

Empathy is another cornerstone of emotional intelligence, enabling you to step outside your own experience and see the world through someone else's eyes. This ability to connect with others on an emotional level is not about solving their problems or agreeing with their perspectives but about acknowledging and validating their feelings. Imagine a friend confiding in you about a difficult day. Empathy involves not just hearing their words but sensing the frustration or sadness beneath them. It's the difference between saying, "That's tough," and truly communicating, "I can see how hard this has been for you." Empathy deepens relationships, builds trust, and fosters a sense of connection that transcends surface-level interactions.

Effective communication is intricately linked to emotional intelligence. It's not just about what you say but how you say it—and how well you listen. Active listening involves giving your full attention to the speaker, seeking to understand rather than simply waiting for your turn to respond. This requires tuning into both verbal and nonverbal cues, such as tone, body language, and facial expressions, which often convey more than words alone. Emotional intelligence also helps you navigate difficult conversations with tact and sensitivity. Instead of reacting defensively to criticism, for example, you might acknowledge the other person's perspective and use it as an opportunity for growth. Clear, compassionate communication fosters mutual understanding and reduces the likelihood of misunderstandings or conflict.

Social awareness extends the principles of self-awareness and empathy to a broader context. It involves reading the emotional tone of a room, recognizing group dynamics, and understanding how your actions affect others. This skill is particularly valuable in professional settings, where navigating relationships with colleagues, clients, or team members requires a nuanced understanding of interpersonal dynamics. A leader with high social awareness, for instance, might notice when a team is feeling demoralized and take steps to address the underlying issues before they escalate. By attuning yourself to the emotions and needs of those around you, you can respond in ways that strengthen relationships and build collaborative environments.

Developing emotional intelligence also requires a commitment to self-reflection and growth. This means being willing to examine your own biases, assumptions, and habits, and to accept feedback from others, even when it's uncomfortable. Self-reflection allows you to identify areas where you may be falling short, such as a tendency to interrupt during conversations or difficulty managing stress. Feedback, when approached with an open mind, provides an external perspective that can highlight blind spots you might not see on your own. Growth in emotional intelligence is not a linear process; it involves ongoing learning, experimentation, and a willingness to adapt.

Resilience is a byproduct of emotional intelligence, equipping you to navigate life's inevitable challenges with grace and perseverance. When faced with setbacks, a person with high emotional intelligence is less likely to be derailed by frustration or self-doubt. Instead, they acknowledge their feelings, seek support if needed, and focus on finding solutions. This resilience is bolstered by a strong sense of self-awareness, which provides clarity in times of uncertainty, and by empathy, which fosters meaningful connections that can serve as sources of strength during difficult periods.

The impact of emotional intelligence extends far beyond individual well-being. In relationships, it creates deeper bonds and reduces conflict, enabling you to navigate differences with understanding and respect. In the workplace, it enhances collaboration, leadership, and the ability to manage stress. On a societal level, it fosters inclusivity, compassion, and the ability to bridge divides. Emotional intelligence is not a luxury or a secondary skill—it is an essential component of living a balanced, fulfilling life.

By committing to the development of emotional intelligence, you unlock not only the ability to understand and manage your emotions but also the capacity to connect with others on a profound level. It is a journey of self-discovery and connection, one that enriches every aspect of your life and empowers you to face challenges with confidence, compassion, and clarity. This ability to navigate the complexities of human emotion is not just a skill but a profound strength, one that lays the foundation for personal and collective growth.

Stress Management Techniques

Stress has a way of infiltrating daily life, often without warning. It builds in the background, triggered by tight deadlines, unexpected changes, or the sheer weight of responsibilities. While a certain level of stress can be motivating, pushing you to meet goals or adapt to challenges, too much of it becomes overwhelming and detrimental. Chronic stress can disrupt sleep, impair focus, and even lead to long-term health issues. Managing stress effectively doesn't mean eliminating it altogether; rather, it's about creating strategies to navigate its effects and maintain balance. By understanding how stress operates and adopting techniques to handle it, you can regain control and cultivate resilience in the face of life's demands.

One of the most effective ways to manage stress is to become attuned to its early signals. Stress often manifests physically, emotionally, or behaviorally before it becomes overwhelming. You might notice tension in your shoulders, a racing heart, or feelings of irritability. These signs are your body's way of alerting you to underlying pressure, urging you to address it before it escalates. Paying attention to these cues allows you to intervene early, preventing stress from taking root. Awareness is the foundation of stress management, as it gives you the clarity to recognize what's happening and the opportunity to take action.

Breathing techniques are a powerful tool for calming the body and mind during moments of stress. When stress triggers the body's fight-or-flight response, your breathing often becomes shallow and rapid, fueling feelings of anxiety. Deep, intentional breathing counteracts this response, signaling to your nervous system that it's safe to relax. A simple practice involves inhaling deeply through your nose for a count of four, holding the breath for four counts, and exhaling slowly through your mouth for a count of six. This rhythmic breathing slows your heart rate and encourages a sense of calm, allowing you to approach challenges with greater clarity.

Physical activity is another highly effective stress management technique. Exercise releases endorphins, the body's natural mood elevators, which help reduce tension and improve your overall sense of well-being. Whether it's a brisk walk, a yoga session, or a more intense workout, moving your body provides an outlet for pent-up energy and redirects your focus. Physical activity also creates a mental break from stressors, offering a chance to reset and approach problems with a fresh perspective. Over time, regular exercise not only alleviates immediate stress but also builds resilience, equipping you to handle future challenges with greater ease.

Time management plays a critical role in reducing stress. Often, stress arises from feeling overwhelmed by a long list of tasks or looming deadlines. Breaking tasks into smaller, manageable steps can make even the most daunting projects feel achievable. Prioritizing your responsibilities, focusing on what is most important, and setting realistic timelines help create structure and reduce the sense of chaos. The act of planning itself can be calming, as it replaces uncertainty with a clear path forward. When you allocate time intentionally and allow for breaks, you create a rhythm that supports productivity without leading to burnout.

Mindfulness is an invaluable practice for managing stress. By bringing your attention to the present moment, mindfulness interrupts the cycle of worry and rumination that often accompanies stress. Stress frequently stems from dwelling on the past or anticipating the future, but mindfulness anchors you in the here and now. Simple practices, such as focusing on the sensations of your breath, noticing the sights and sounds around you, or savoring a meal, help cultivate this awareness. Over time, mindfulness strengthens your ability to respond to stress with calmness and intention rather than reacting impulsively.

Another powerful stress management technique is cultivating a strong support system. Sharing your thoughts and feelings with trusted friends, family members, or colleagues can lighten the emotional load and offer new perspectives on a situation. Talking through challenges often clarifies them, making solutions more apparent. Beyond conversations, simply spending time with supportive people can boost your mood and remind you that you're not alone in facing stress. These connections act as a buffer against the isolating effects of stress, providing a sense of belonging and reassurance.

Engaging in activities that bring joy or relaxation can also help alleviate stress. Creative outlets, such as painting, writing, or playing music, channel your energy into something constructive and fulfilling. Similarly, hobbies like gardening, cooking, or reading offer a welcome distraction and create moments of pleasure in your day. These activities serve as a reminder that there is more to life than stressors, allowing you to reconnect with the things that bring you happiness and meaning. Incorporating these moments regularly nourishes your spirit and maintains balance.

Sleep is a fundamental yet often overlooked component of stress management. Chronic stress can disrupt sleep patterns, leading to a vicious cycle where poor sleep intensifies stress and vice versa. Prioritizing restful sleep by maintaining a consistent bedtime, creating a calming pre-sleep routine, and minimizing screen time in the evening helps regulate your body's rhythms. Quality sleep restores your energy, sharpens your focus, and enhances your ability to cope with challenges. It is during sleep that your body and mind recover, making it an essential element of resilience.

Gratitude also plays a surprising role in managing stress. Taking time to reflect on the positives in your life shifts your focus away from what's causing stress and onto what's going well. This practice doesn't diminish the reality of challenges but provides a counterbalance, fostering optimism and perspective. Writing down a few things you're grateful for each day creates a habit of noticing and appreciating the good, which can help mitigate the effects of stress over time.

Stress is an inevitable part of life, but it doesn't have to control you. By building a toolkit of techniques—ranging from breathing exercises and physical activity to mindfulness and emotional support—you can navigate stress with greater confidence and ease. Each method offers a unique way to counteract the pressures of daily life, allowing you to regain balance and maintain well-being. The key is to experiment with these approaches and find what resonates most with you, creating a personalized strategy for managing stress in a way that empowers and sustains you.

The Art of Bouncing Back

Resilience is often described as the ability to bounce back from setbacks, but it is so much more than simply recovering from hardship. It is the art of adapting, growing, and finding strength in adversity. Life's challenges often arrive unannounced, disrupting plans, testing limits, and sometimes leaving scars. Yet, within every setback lies the potential for renewal and growth, a chance to reimagine what is possible. The art of bouncing back is not about avoiding difficulty or pretending it doesn't hurt; it's about embracing the struggle, learning from it, and emerging stronger and more focused than before.

Setbacks have a way of shaking the foundation of who you believe you are and what you think you're capable of. They can make even the most confident person question their abilities and wonder if they have what it takes to move forward. However, while setbacks are unavoidable, how you respond to them is entirely within your control. This response begins with acknowledging the reality of the situation. Denying or minimizing a problem doesn't make it go away; in fact, it often prolongs the pain. Facing the truth head-on, no matter how uncomfortable, lays the groundwork for recovery.

It is natural to feel a wave of emotions when dealing with a setback. Anger, frustration, sadness, or even guilt may surface, and these feelings can be overwhelming. Yet, suppressing them only leads to further emotional strain. Allowing yourself to feel and process these emotions is an essential step in bouncing back. By accepting your feelings without judgment, you create the emotional space to begin healing. This doesn't mean dwelling on negativity but rather giving yourself permission to experience the full range of emotions before focusing on solutions.

Perspective is a powerful tool in the face of adversity. When a setback occurs, it can feel like the end of the road, as though the entire world has collapsed around you. But often, stepping back and reframing the situation reveals a broader view. Consider the story of someone who loses their job—a devastating blow in the moment. Yet, for many, this loss becomes the catalyst for pursuing a long-held dream, discovering a new passion, or finding a role that aligns better with their values. The ability to see setbacks as temporary and as opportunities for growth is what separates those who remain stuck from those who rise stronger.

Resilience doesn't mean weathering the storm alone; it often requires the courage to seek support. Sharing your burden with trusted friends, family, or colleagues can provide comfort and perspective. Sometimes, hearing someone else's story of overcoming similar challenges is enough to remind you that setbacks are a shared human experience, not an isolated failure. Support networks also offer practical help, whether it's guidance, resources, or simply a listening ear. The act of reaching out, of letting others into your struggle, reinforces the idea that you don't have to face difficulties in solitude.

Adversity has a way of teaching lessons that success often cannot. Each setback carries with it an opportunity to reflect and grow. Taking the time to analyze what went wrong, what could have been done differently, and what factors were beyond your control turns failure into a learning experience. This reflection isn't about assigning blame but about gaining insight. Perhaps a missed opportunity was due to poor time management, or a relationship faltered due to miscommunication. By identifying these lessons, you equip yourself with the tools to approach future challenges with greater wisdom and preparation.

Action is the bridge between reflection and recovery. Once the lessons from a setback have been gathered, the next step is to apply them. This might mean setting new goals, developing a different strategy, or building habits that prevent similar setbacks in the future. The key is to start small, focusing on immediate, achievable steps that create momentum. Action not only propels you forward but also rebuilds confidence, reminding you that progress is possible even in the wake of difficulty. Each small success reinforces your belief in your ability to overcome challenges, creating a positive cycle of growth and achievement.

Resilience is also deeply tied to self-compassion. It's easy to be hard on yourself after a setback, to replay mistakes in your mind or criticize your perceived shortcomings. Yet, this self-criticism only adds to the weight of the challenge. Treating yourself with kindness and understanding, as you would a friend facing a similar situation, shifts the focus from blame to healing. Self-compassion allows you to acknowledge your humanity, to recognize that everyone stumbles, and to forgive yourself for imperfections. This gentle approach creates a foundation of self-worth that supports resilience and recovery.

The ability to bounce back is not something you are born with; it is a skill honed through experience and intentional effort. Each time you face a setback and rise again, you strengthen this skill, building a reservoir of resilience that serves you in future challenges. Over time, you learn to trust not in the absence of adversity but in your ability to navigate it.

This trust becomes a source of inner strength, a quiet confidence that empowers you to take risks, pursue goals, and embrace life's uncertainties.

Adversity, while difficult, often reveals the depths of your character and the extent of your capabilities. It strips away pretense and forces you to confront what truly matters. In the process, it shapes you into a version of yourself that is more grounded, more empathetic, and more resilient. The art of bouncing back is not a rejection of struggle but an embrace of its transformative power. It is the realization that setbacks, no matter how painful, are not the end of the story. They are simply a chapter—one that, with the right mindset and effort, can lead to a narrative of strength, growth, and renewed purpose.

Creating Mental Toughness

Mental toughness is the ability to remain focused, calm, and resilient in the face of challenges, setbacks, and pressure. It is not simply a trait you are born with, but a skill that can be cultivated through experience, practice, and intentional effort. People who possess mental toughness are not immune to stress, fear, or doubt; rather, they have developed the capacity to manage these emotions effectively and push forward regardless of the circumstances. This quality is the foundation for achieving long-term goals, overcoming adversity, and maintaining a sense of purpose even when the odds are stacked against you.

At its core, mental toughness begins with a strong sense of self-belief. This belief is not arrogance or blind optimism but a deep, unwavering confidence in your ability to navigate challenges and adapt to changing circumstances. Self-belief is built over time through small victories and a willingness to step outside your comfort zone. Each time you confront a fear, take a risk, or achieve something you once thought was beyond your reach, you reinforce the belief that you are capable of more than you imagined. This belief becomes the cornerstone of mental toughness, providing a steady foundation even when external circumstances are uncertain or difficult.

The ability to set and maintain clear goals is another essential component of mental toughness. When you have a well-defined purpose, it becomes easier to stay focused and motivated, even in the face of distractions or setbacks. Goals act as a compass, guiding your actions and decisions. However, mental toughness requires more than just setting goals—it demands the discipline to stick to them, even when the initial excitement fades or when progress feels slow. This discipline comes from a deep connection to your "why," the underlying reason for pursuing your goals. When your purpose is meaningful and aligned with your values, it becomes a source of strength that sustains you through challenges.

One of the most challenging aspects of developing mental toughness is learning to embrace discomfort. Growth rarely occurs within the confines of comfort; it is born out of struggle, effort, and the willingness to endure temporary pain for long-term gain. Whether it's pushing through a difficult workout, tackling a complex project, or confronting a personal fear, leaning into discomfort teaches you that you are stronger than you think. Each time you face a challenge head-on, you expand your capacity to handle adversity, building the resilience that is essential for mental toughness.

Emotional regulation plays a critical role in maintaining mental toughness. Life is full of situations that can trigger anger, frustration, or self-doubt, and these emotions, if left unchecked, can derail your focus and decision-making. Mental toughness involves recognizing these emotions as they arise and managing them in a way that keeps you grounded. This doesn't mean suppressing your feelings but rather channeling them in constructive ways. For example, anger can be transformed into determination, and fear can become a signal to prepare more thoroughly. By developing the ability to stay calm under pressure, you create a mental space where clarity and rational thinking can thrive.

A key aspect of mental toughness is the ability to control your attention. In a world filled with distractions, staying focused on what truly matters is increasingly difficult but incredibly important. Mental toughness involves training your mind to prioritize what is within your control and to let go of what isn't. This requires a deliberate effort to avoid wasting energy on external factors, such as other people's opinions or the unpredictability of outcomes. By narrowing your focus to the tasks and decisions that are directly within your power, you conserve mental energy and maintain a sense of agency.

The role of setbacks in building mental toughness cannot be overstated. Setbacks, though painful, are some of the most effective teachers. They reveal gaps in your preparation, highlight areas for growth, and test your commitment to your goals. Mentally tough individuals view setbacks not as failures but as opportunities to learn and improve. They analyze what went wrong, adapt their approach, and return to the challenge with renewed determination. This mindset transforms obstacles into stepping stones, allowing you to grow stronger with each experience.

Self-talk is another powerful tool in cultivating mental toughness. The way you speak to yourself, especially in moments of difficulty, can either build you up or tear you down. Negative self-talk—statements like "I can't do this" or "I'm not good enough"—undermines your confidence and creates unnecessary barriers. Mentally tough individuals practice positive, constructive self-talk, reminding themselves of their strengths, past successes, and ability to overcome challenges. This internal dialogue is not about ignoring reality but about framing it in a way that empowers rather than discourages. Replacing doubt with determination and fear with focus fuels the perseverance needed to push through obstacles.

Adaptability is another hallmark of mental toughness. Life rarely goes as planned, and the ability to adjust your approach without losing sight of your goals is crucial. Mentally tough individuals are flexible in their strategies but firm in their purpose. They understand that setbacks, detours, and unexpected changes are inevitable, and they respond with creativity and resilience. This adaptability allows them to remain effective and composed, even in unpredictable situations, turning challenges into opportunities for growth.

The journey to mental toughness is not easy, but it is profoundly rewarding. It requires consistent effort, self-reflection, and a willingness to face challenges with courage and determination. Each step forward, no matter how small, strengthens your resilience and prepares you for the next test. Over time, mental toughness becomes a way of life—a mindset that empowers you to pursue your goals with unwavering focus and to embrace life's uncertainties with confidence and grace. It is not the absence of struggle but the ability to thrive in its presence that defines true mental toughness.

Chapter 4: Harnessing Your Inner Power

Understanding Personal Energy

Energy is the invisible currency of life, a vital force that drives every thought, decision, and action. It is not merely a physical resource, like the stamina needed to climb a staircase, but a multi-dimensional system encompassing mental, emotional, and spiritual reserves. Personal energy shapes how you show up in the world—how you connect with others, tackle challenges, and pursue your goals. It is finite yet renewable, fragile yet powerful. Understanding personal energy requires becoming aware of its sources, recognizing when it is depleted, and learning how to restore and maintain it to thrive in every aspect of life.

Life often feels like a balancing act between the demands of work, relationships, and personal growth. These demands pull on your energy, sometimes to the point where you feel drained and unable to function at your best. The first step toward managing your personal energy is understanding where it comes from and how it flows through your life. Physical energy, the most easily understood form, originates from how you care for your body. It is influenced by sleep, nutrition, and movement. A well-rested body fueled by wholesome food and regular activity is a foundation for vitality. Sleep, in particular, is essential. It is during rest that your body repairs itself and your mind processes the events of the day, preparing you to face new challenges.

Mental energy is a different dimension, tied to your ability to focus, solve problems, and make decisions. It is often expended in environments that require sustained attention or multitasking. The modern world, with its constant notifications and endless streams of information, can be especially taxing on mental reserves. Emotional energy, on the other hand, governs how you feel and react to the world around you. Emotions, whether positive or negative, are powerful energy drivers. A joyful experience can uplift and energize you, while prolonged stress or conflict can leave you feeling utterly drained. Spiritual energy, though more abstract, is equally important. It reflects your sense of purpose and connection to something greater than yourself, whether that's a community, a set of values, or a belief system.

Energy depletion is often gradual, creeping in as you juggle responsibilities and push through fatigue without pause. Over time, this can lead to burnout, a state where even the simplest tasks feel insurmountable. Recognizing the signs of low energy is crucial. Physically, this might manifest as persistent tiredness or frequent illness. Mentally, it could show up as difficulty concentrating or making decisions. Emotionally, you might notice irritability, apathy, or a sense of being overwhelmed. Spiritually, you could feel disconnected or lacking in purpose. These symptoms are signals that your energy reserves are running low and that it's time to recharge.

Replenishing personal energy requires intentional practices tailored to each dimension. Physically, this might mean prioritizing quality sleep and nourishing your body with balanced meals. Movement, whether it's a brisk walk, yoga, or dancing, invigorates the body and clears the mind. Mentally, taking breaks from screens, setting boundaries around work, and engaging in activities that stimulate creativity can restore focus. Emotionally, connecting with loved ones, practicing gratitude, or seeking therapy provides an outlet for processing feelings and replenishing emotional reserves. Spiritually, engaging in practices like meditation, prayer, or spending time in nature can rekindle a sense of purpose and connection.

It's also important to recognize the role of energy leaks—habits, environments, or relationships that drain energy unnecessarily. These can be subtle, like spending hours scrolling through social media, or more significant, like staying in a toxic relationship or working in an unfulfilling job. Identifying and addressing these energy leaks is as important as replenishing energy. It enables you to conserve your reserves and direct them toward activities and relationships that align with your values and goals.

Energy is not just about managing depletion and restoration; it's also about flow. When energy flows freely, you experience a state of alignment and ease, often referred to as being "in the zone" or "in flow." This state occurs when your actions are fully aligned with your values and you are deeply engaged in the present moment. Achieving this flow often requires clarity about what matters most to you and a willingness to let go of distractions or obligations that do not serve your higher purpose. It is in this state of alignment that energy becomes a source of joy and fulfillment rather than a finite resource to be rationed.

Understanding personal energy also involves recognizing its cyclical nature. Just as the seasons change, your energy levels fluctuate throughout the day, week, or month. Some people feel most energized in the morning, while others hit their stride in the evening. Honoring these natural rhythms allows you to align your most demanding tasks with your peak energy periods, maximizing productivity and minimizing frustration. Similarly, recognizing when you need rest or downtime helps you avoid pushing through exhaustion, which only compounds depletion.

Energy is deeply interconnected with the people and environments around you. The company you keep can either uplift and energize you or drain and exhaust you. Surrounding yourself with positive, supportive individuals creates an exchange of energy that is mutually beneficial. Similarly, the spaces you inhabit—your home, workplace, or even the natural environment—affect your energy levels. Cluttered, chaotic spaces can feel draining, while organized, peaceful environments foster a sense of calm and renewal. Cultivating relationships and environments that support your cnergy is an essential part of maintaining balance.

The Science of Motivation

Motivation is the invisible force that propels human behavior, driving individuals to pursue goals, overcome obstacles, and achieve growth. It shapes the way people act, think, and respond to life's challenges, yet its nature is far from static. It ebbs and flows, influenced by internal desires, external circumstances, and biological mechanisms. Understanding the science behind motivation provides valuable insights into what drives action and how to cultivate the persistence needed to turn aspirations into reality.

At its most fundamental level, motivation can be categorized into two distinct types: intrinsic and extrinsic. Intrinsic motivation arises from within, fueled by personal interest, curiosity, or a deep sense of purpose. It is the reason someone might spend hours mastering an instrument, not for an audience but for the sheer joy of creating music. Extrinsic motivation, on the other hand, comes from external rewards or pressures, such as earning a promotion, receiving recognition, or avoiding negative consequences. Both forms of motivation have their place, but they operate differently and yield varying outcomes. Intrinsic motivation often leads to long-term satisfaction and creativity, while extrinsic motivation can be effective for achieving short-term goals or meeting external expectations.

The brain plays a central role in regulating motivation, particularly through the release of dopamine, a neurotransmitter often associated with pleasure and reward. When you anticipate or achieve something desirable, such as completing an important task or enjoying a meal, your brain releases dopamine, reinforcing the behavior and encouraging you to repeat it. This reward system is a key driver of motivation, but it is also susceptible to being hijacked by instant gratification. Activities like scrolling through social media or indulging in junk food provide quick dopamine hits, which can diminish the appeal of pursuing longer-term, more meaningful goals. Understanding this dynamic helps explain why motivation can sometimes feel elusive, especially in the face of distractions.

Goals are a cornerstone of motivation, providing direction and purpose. However, not all goals are created equal. Research shows that specific, measurable, and challenging goals are more motivating than vague or easily attainable ones. For example, deciding to "run a 5K in under 30 minutes by the end of the month" provides a clear target and timeline, making it easier to track progress and stay committed. In contrast, a goal like "get in shape" lacks the structure and specificity needed to sustain motivation. Breaking larger goals into smaller, manageable steps further enhances motivation by creating a series of achievable milestones. Each small victory builds confidence and momentum, reinforcing the belief that the ultimate goal is within reach.

The concept of self-efficacy, introduced by psychologist Albert Bandura, is another critical factor in motivation. Self-efficacy refers to your belief in your ability to succeed in a specific task or situation. When you believe you can achieve something, you're more likely to put in the effort and persist in the face of challenges. Conversely, doubt in your abilities can undermine motivation, leading to procrastination or avoidance. Building self-efficacy involves setting realistic goals, celebrating progress, and reflecting on past successes. Each accomplishment, no matter how small, strengthens your confidence and fuels your motivation to take on greater challenges.

Another key aspect of motivation is the interplay between autonomy and accountability. Autonomy—the sense of having control over your actions and decisions—is a powerful motivator. When you feel that you are pursuing a goal because it aligns with your values and interests, rather than because someone else expects it of you, you are more likely to stay engaged and committed. At the same time, accountability can provide the structure and support needed to maintain motivation. Sharing your goals with a trusted friend, mentor, or coach creates a sense of responsibility, as knowing someone else is invested in your progress can push you to follow through even when motivation wanes.

Habits play a crucial role in sustaining motivation over the long term. Motivation is often strongest at the beginning of a new endeavor, but it naturally diminishes over time as the novelty wears off or obstacles arise. Habits bridge the gap between initial enthusiasm and lasting achievement by automating behavior. When an action becomes habitual, it requires less conscious effort and is more likely to be sustained even when motivation is low. For example, establishing a daily routine of writing for 30 minutes can help an aspiring author make steady progress on a novel, regardless of whether they feel particularly inspired on any given day. Building habits involves consistency and repetition, turning deliberate actions into automatic patterns.

The environment also plays a significant role in shaping motivation. A supportive, organized, and inspiring environment can make it easier to stay focused and energized, while a chaotic or negative environment can sap motivation and lead to procrastination. For instance, a clutter-free workspace with minimal distractions fosters productivity, while a noisy or disorganized setting can make it difficult to concentrate. Surrounding yourself with positive influences, such as like-minded peers or mentors, further enhances motivation by creating a network of support and encouragement. The environment you create, both physical and social, can either amplify or undermine your efforts to stay motivated.

Resilience is an often-overlooked component of motivation. Even with the best intentions and plans, setbacks are inevitable. The ability to recover from disappointment, learn from failure, and adapt to changing circumstances is what allows motivation to endure over time. This resilience is rooted in a growth mindset—the belief that abilities and intelligence can be developed through effort and learning. When you view challenges as opportunities for growth rather than as insurmountable barriers, you are more likely to persevere and maintain motivation, even in the face of adversity.

Cultivating Inner Strength

Inner strength is the quiet resilience that anchors you in the face of life's uncertainties. It is not loud or boastful but steady and enduring, a foundation that enables you to navigate challenges, make tough decisions, and remain true to yourself. Unlike physical strength, which is visible and tangible, inner strength is invisible yet profoundly impactful, shaping your thoughts, actions, and reactions. It is a resource you can draw upon in moments of conflict, adversity, or doubt—a source of stability that allows you to persevere when everything else feels unsteady. Cultivating it requires intentionality, self-awareness, and a commitment to growth, but its rewards are immeasurable.

One of the first steps in building inner strength is understanding your values. These are the principles that guide your decisions and define what truly matters to you. When you have clarity about your values, you create a compass that helps you navigate even the most difficult situations. For example, someone who values integrity will find strength in being honest, even when it's uncomfortable or inconvenient. Similarly, a person who prioritizes kindness may draw on their inner strength to show compassion, even in the face of hostility. Knowing your values provides a sense of direction and purpose, grounding you in what is meaningful and helping you stay aligned with your true self.

Inner strength also grows through self-awareness, the ability to recognize and understand your thoughts, emotions, and behaviors. Often, people move through life on autopilot, reacting to situations without fully understanding why they feel or act the way they do. Self-awareness breaks this cycle, allowing you to pause, reflect, and choose your responses deliberately. For instance, when faced with criticism, a self-aware person might recognize the initial sting of hurt or defensiveness but choose not to let those feelings dictate their reaction. Instead, they might reflect on whether the criticism holds any truth and respond constructively. This capacity to observe and manage your inner world is a hallmark of inner strength, enabling you to remain composed and thoughtful even in emotionally charged situations.

Resilience is another cornerstone of inner strength. Life is unpredictable, and setbacks are inevitable, but resilience allows you to adapt, recover, and move forward. It is not about avoiding pain or pretending that challenges don't exist; rather, it is about acknowledging difficulties while refusing to let them define you. Resilient individuals view setbacks as opportunities for growth, using them to learn, refine their approach, and build greater confidence in their ability to overcome obstacles. This mindset doesn't come naturally to everyone, but it can be cultivated through practice. Each time you face adversity and choose to persist, you strengthen your resilience, adding another layer to your inner foundation.

Self-compassion plays a pivotal role in cultivating inner strength. Often, people are their own harshest critics, berating themselves for mistakes or perceived shortcomings. This inner dialogue can erode confidence and make it difficult to move forward. Self-compassion, on the other hand, involves treating yourself with the same kindness and understanding you would offer a friend. It means acknowledging your humanity, recognizing that everyone struggles and stumbles at times, and giving yourself permission to learn and grow without judgment. Far from being a sign of weakness, self-compassion is a source of strength that allows you to bounce back from failure and approach challenges with greater courage and resilience.

Boundaries are another essential aspect of inner strength. These are the limits you set to protect your time, energy, and well-being. Without boundaries, it's easy to become overwhelmed or taken advantage of, leaving you feeling depleted and disconnected from yourself. Setting boundaries requires clarity about your needs and the courage to communicate them, even when it's uncomfortable. For example, saying no to an additional work project might feel difficult in the moment, but it preserves your energy for the commitments that matter most. Boundaries are not about shutting people out; they are about creating the space you need to thrive, allowing you to give your best to yourself and others.

Perspective is a powerful tool for cultivating inner strength. When you're in the midst of a difficult situation, it's easy to feel consumed by it, as though it's the only thing that matters. Stepping back and viewing the situation in the broader context of your life can provide a sense of relief and clarity. For instance, a missed opportunity might feel devastating in the moment, but when viewed through the lens of your long-term goals and experiences, it may reveal itself as a temporary setback rather than a defining failure. Perspective helps you maintain balance, reminding you that challenges are a part of life's ebb and flow, not its entirety.

Trusting yourself is another critical element of inner strength. This trust is built through experience, by taking risks, making decisions, and learning from the outcomes. Each time you listen to your intuition, follow through on a commitment, or navigate a tough situation, you reinforce your belief in your own capabilities. This self-trust becomes a wellspring of confidence, allowing you to face uncertainty with a sense of steadiness. It doesn't mean you'll always have the right answers, but it means you trust your ability to figure things out as you go.

Inner strength thrives in moments of stillness. In today's fast-paced world, where distractions abound and productivity often takes precedence, finding time to pause and reflect can feel like a luxury. Yet, it is in these quiet moments that you reconnect with yourself, process your emotions, and gain clarity about what truly matters. Whether through meditation, journaling, or simply sitting in silence, creating space for stillness allows you to recharge and strengthen your inner foundation.

At its essence, inner strength is about cultivating a relationship with yourself—knowing who you are, what you stand for, and what you need to thrive. It is not a destination but an ongoing journey, one that requires patience, self-compassion, and a willingness to grow. Each step you take to build your inner strength, no matter how small, contributes to a life that feels more grounded, purposeful, and resilient. It is this strength that enables you to face life's challenges with grace and courage, transforming obstacles into opportunities and uncertainty into growth.

Unlocking Creative Potential

Creativity is often imagined as a mysterious gift, something reserved for artists, writers, or inventors.

But creativity is not confined to a select few—it is an innate human trait, a powerful tool that can be cultivated and applied to every area of life. Whether you are solving a complex problem, designing a new product, or simply finding a fresh approach to a daily routine, creativity is the spark that drives innovation and originality. Unlocking your creative potential is not about waiting for inspiration to strike; it's about creating the conditions in which imagination and ingenuity can flourish.

The foundation of creative potential lies in curiosity. It is the drive to ask questions, explore new ideas, and challenge assumptions. Curiosity transforms the mundane into the extraordinary, allowing you to see possibilities that others might overlook. Consider how children approach the world—with an endless stream of "why" and "what if" questions. This natural curiosity is the birthplace of creativity, yet many adults lose touch with it as they grow older, constrained by routines, responsibilities, or a fear of failure. Reawakening curiosity begins with giving yourself permission to wonder, to explore topics outside your expertise, and to approach the world with a beginner's mind. When you embrace curiosity, you open the door to creative thinking.

Exposure to diverse experiences, perspectives, and ideas is another critical element in unlocking creativity. The mind thrives on novelty, and the more varied your environment, the more raw material your brain has to work with. Consider how breakthroughs often come from unexpected connections between seemingly unrelated fields. A musician inspired by architecture, a scientist borrowing techniques from art, or an entrepreneur blending technology with psychology—these intersections are where innovation often takes root. Seeking out new experiences, whether by reading widely, traveling, or engaging with people who have different backgrounds, expands your mental landscape and provides the seeds from which creative ideas can grow.

Constraints, counterintuitively, can also enhance creativity. While it might seem that complete freedom would fuel the greatest innovation, research shows that limitations often inspire more inventive solutions. When resources, time, or materials are restricted, the mind is forced to think more inventively, finding ways to work within or around those boundaries. For example, some of history's most iconic artworks or technological achievements were born from adversity or scarcity, proving that constraints are not obstacles but opportunities to push the boundaries of possibility. Embracing limitations as a challenge rather than a hindrance can lead to unexpected breakthroughs.

The creative process thrives on playfulness. Taking yourself too seriously can stifle imagination, as the pressure to be "right" or "perfect" creates mental blocks. Play, on the other hand, encourages experimentation and risk-taking, essential components of creativity. Think of how children play with building blocks, trying countless combinations without fear of failure. They are not worried about the end result; they are absorbed in the act of creation itself. Adults can benefit from this same mindset. Approaching challenges with a sense of play allows you to explore ideas without judgment, fostering the kind of free-flowing thought that leads to innovation.

Failure, far from being the enemy of creativity, is one of its most valuable tools. Every misstep, mistake, or dead-end is an opportunity to learn, refine, and approach a problem from a new angle. Many of the world's greatest innovators attribute their success to their willingness to fail repeatedly. Thomas Edison famously remarked that he didn't fail 10,000 times when inventing the light bulb; he simply found 10,000 ways that didn't work. This resilience is at the heart of unlocking creative potential. When you view failure not as a verdict on your abilities but as a natural part of the creative process, you free yourself to take risks, experiment, and push boundaries.

The environment in which you work also plays a significant role in fostering creativity. A cluttered, chaotic space may feel overwhelming, while a sterile, uninspiring setting can stifle imaginative thought. Creating a space that energizes and inspires you is essential. This doesn't mean you need a lavish studio or a perfect setup; it could be as simple as a corner filled with objects that spark joy or a playlist that helps you focus. Surrounding yourself with beauty, inspiration, and tools that invite exploration builds an atmosphere where ideas can flourish. Equally important is giving yourself uninterrupted time to dive deeply into a project. Creativity often requires sustained focus, and carving out time to immerse yourself fully can lead to breakthroughs.

One of the most underrated aspects of creativity is the ability to step away from the problem at hand. When you hit a mental block, walking away can be more effective than forcing a solution. This phenomenon, known as the "incubation effect," occurs when you take a break and allow your subconscious mind to process the problem. Have you ever noticed how ideas seem to strike when you're in the shower, taking a walk, or drifting off to sleep? These moments of clarity often come because you've given your mind the space to wander, allowing connections to form organically. Embracing periods of rest and reflection is as vital to creativity as active effort.

Collaboration is another powerful way to unlock creative potential. While creativity is often imagined as a solitary pursuit, it can be amplified through the exchange of ideas with others. Working with people who think differently challenges your assumptions and introduces perspectives you may not have considered. Brainstorming sessions, collaborative projects, or simply sharing your thoughts with a trusted friend can spark unexpected solutions. The key is to approach collaboration with openness and humility, recognizing that the best ideas often emerge from collective effort rather than individual brilliance.

Chapter 5: Creating Meaningful Goals

The Art of Goal Setting

Goal setting is a transformative practice, a deliberate act of crafting a vision for the future and creating a roadmap to reach it. It is more than simply deciding what you want; it is about defining purpose, channeling focus, and committing to steady progress. Goals give structure to dreams, turning abstract desires into actionable steps. They provide clarity, direction, and the motivation to persevere, even when the journey becomes arduous. Mastering the art of goal setting requires not only understanding the mechanics of the process but also cultivating the mindset and discipline necessary to bring those aspirations to life.

Clarity is the foundation of effective goal setting. Vague or ambiguous goals are like trying to navigate a city without a map; you may move in circles without ever reaching your destination. Instead, goals should be specific and concrete, leaving no room for misinterpretation. For example, aspiring to "be healthier" is admirable but lacks the precision needed for actionable steps. Defining the goal as "exercise for 30 minutes five times a week" transforms it into a clear, measurable target. This specificity allows you to track progress, which is essential for maintaining momentum and staying accountable.

Understanding why a goal matters is equally critical. The "why" serves as the emotional anchor, the deeper reason behind the pursuit. Goals rooted in external validation or societal expectations often lose their appeal over time, as they fail to resonate on a personal level. In contrast, goals aligned with your values and passions create a sense of intrinsic motivation. Consider someone pursuing a career change. If their motivation is solely financial, they may struggle to endure the challenges of starting over. However, if the goal is driven by a desire to find fulfilling work that aligns with their purpose, they are far more likely to stay the course. Connecting goals to meaning transforms them from obligations into opportunities for growth and self-expression.

Breaking goals into smaller, manageable steps is a powerful strategy for maintaining focus and reducing overwhelm. Big dreams can feel intimidating, making it tempting to procrastinate or abandon them altogether. By dividing a goal into incremental milestones, you create a series of achievable victories that build confidence and momentum. For instance, writing a book may seem daunting, but committing to writing 500 words a day feels far more attainable. Each step forward, no matter how small, reinforces the belief that the larger goal is within reach. This approach not only simplifies the process but also provides regular opportunities to celebrate progress, fueling further motivation.

Flexibility is another key aspect of successful goal setting. Life is unpredictable, and rigid plans can quickly become obsolete in the face of unexpected circumstances. Goals should serve as guides, not constraints, allowing room for adaptation and growth. Sometimes, the path to achieving a goal may need to change, or the goal itself may evolve as new insights emerge. For example, someone pursuing a fitness goal might initially aim to run a marathon but later discover a passion for cycling. Adjusting the goal to align with this newfound interest ensures it remains meaningful and sustainable. Flexibility is not a sign of failure but a recognition that growth is a dynamic process.

Accountability is a powerful force in goal achievement. Sharing your goals with someone you trust, whether a friend, mentor, or coach, creates a sense of responsibility that can keep you on track. When others are aware of your intentions, you are more likely to follow through, not just for yourself but also because you don't want to disappoint those who believe in you. Furthermore, having someone to discuss progress, challenges, and successes with provides invaluable support and perspective. Accountability partners can offer encouragement during difficult times and celebrate milestones, reinforcing your commitment to the goal.

The role of visualization in goal setting cannot be overstated. Imagining yourself achieving your goal creates a mental picture that reinforces your belief in its possibility. This practice, often used by athletes, helps bridge the gap between where you are and where you want to be. Visualization not only motivates but also prepares your mind for success. For example, a musician preparing for a performance might visualize themselves playing confidently on stage, hearing the applause and feeling the satisfaction of a job well done. This mental rehearsal builds confidence and reduces anxiety, making the actual achievement feel more attainable.

One of the most overlooked aspects of goal setting is the balance between ambition and realism. While it's important to aim high, setting goals that are entirely out of reach can lead to frustration and discouragement. The best goals challenge you to grow while remaining achievable with effort and persistence. For instance, aiming to double your income in a month may not be realistic, but developing a plan to increase your earning potential over a year strikes a balance between aspiration and feasibility. Finding this equilibrium ensures that goals inspire rather than intimidate, keeping you engaged and motivated.

Celebrating progress is an essential yet often neglected component of goal setting. Many people focus so intently on the end result that they overlook the milestones along the way. Taking time to acknowledge and reward your efforts reinforces positive behavior and reminds you of how far you've come. Whether it's treating yourself to something special or simply reflecting on your accomplishments, these moments of recognition build confidence and sustain motivation. They also make the journey itself more enjoyable, transforming the pursuit of a goal into a source of fulfillment rather than a relentless chase.

The art of goal setting is not a one-size-fits-all process. It requires introspection, experimentation, and a willingness to learn from both successes and setbacks. Each goal you set and pursue teaches you something about yourself—your values, your strengths, and your capacity for growth. By approaching goals with clarity, intention, and resilience, you create a framework for turning aspirations into achievements. Goal setting is not just about reaching a destination; it is about the person you become in the process, the skills you develop, and the insights you gain along the way. It is a practice that empowers you to shape your life with purpose and intention, unlocking your potential to achieve far more than you ever thought possible.

Aligning Goals with Values

Understanding the connection between your goals and your values is one of the most profound steps you can take toward living a fulfilled and intentional life. Goals that are misaligned with your core values often feel hollow, even when you achieve them. They can create a sense of dissatisfaction or confusion, leaving you wondering why success didn't bring the joy or meaning you anticipated. When goals and values are in harmony, however, they fuel a sense of purpose that drives motivation and fosters a deeper sense of well-being. Aligning the two creates a life that feels coherent and authentic, where every step forward resonates with what truly matters to you.

Values are the guiding principles that define who you are and what you stand for. They reflect what you prioritize and what gives your life meaning. For some, values might center on family, creativity, or compassion, while for others they might emphasize independence, achievement, or adventure. These principles act as an internal compass, shaping your decisions and providing clarity during moments of uncertainty. However, values are not always as apparent as we might think. Many people go through life adopting the values of their environment—whether from family, culture, or society—without questioning whether they truly reflect their own aspirations. Discovering your authentic values requires introspection and an honest evaluation of what brings you fulfillment and joy.

When setting goals, it's easy to become preoccupied with external expectations. Society often defines success in terms of wealth, status, or achievement, and it can be tempting to adopt these markers as your own. For example, striving for a promotion at work might seem like an obvious goal, but if it requires sacrificing family time and your core value is connection, the achievement may feel bittersweet. Similarly, pursuing a goal because it looks impressive on paper—such as starting a business or running a marathon—might not deliver satisfaction if it isn't tied to something you genuinely care about. These external influences can cloud your judgment, leading you to pursue goals that are out of sync with your values.

Aligning goals with values begins with a process of self-reflection. Take time to examine what truly matters to you, not what others expect of you or what you think you should value. Reflect on moments in your life when you felt the most fulfilled, energized, or proud. What was happening during those times, and what did those experiences have in common? Were you helping others, expressing creativity, or challenging yourself in meaningful ways? Identifying these patterns can reveal the core values that underpin your sense of purpose. Once you have clarity about your values, you can use them as a filter for evaluating potential goals.

A goal that aligns with your values will often feel energizing, even if it challenges you. For example, if one of your core values is growth, you might feel excited about taking on a goal that pushes you outside your comfort zone, such as learning a new skill or tackling a difficult project. On the other hand, a goal that conflicts with your values may leave you feeling uneasy or disconnected, even if it seems appealing on the surface. For instance, if freedom is a core value, committing to a rigid schedule or a highly structured career path might feel stifling, no matter how much external reward it offers. Listening to these emotional cues can help you discern whether a goal truly aligns with your deeper priorities.

Sometimes, the process of aligning goals with values requires making difficult choices. You may find that certain goals, while meaningful, come into conflict with one another. For instance, you might value both financial security and adventure, but pursuing a high-paying job could limit your ability to travel or explore new experiences. In such cases, it's important to prioritize. Ask yourself which value feels more pressing or closely tied to your long-term happiness. This doesn't mean abandoning one value entirely, but rather finding a way to strike a balance. Perhaps you could pursue a job that allows for remote work, enabling you to fulfill both values in different ways.

Aligning goals with values also requires patience and adaptability. Values often remain constant, but the way you express them through your goals may evolve over time. For example, someone who values contribution might initially pursue a career in social work but later decide to start a nonprofit organization. Both paths honor the same core value, but the goals shift to reflect new circumstances, experiences, or ambitions. Being open to this evolution ensures that your goals remain relevant and meaningful throughout the different stages of your life.

It's worth noting that aligning goals with values doesn't guarantee an easy path. In fact, pursuing a goal that truly reflects your values may require more effort and commitment than chasing a superficial or externally motivated target. For instance, someone who values creativity might face challenges in establishing themselves as an artist, while someone who values justice might encounter resistance when advocating for social change. However, the sense of fulfillment that comes from living in alignment with your values can sustain you through these difficulties. Knowing that your actions are rooted in what genuinely matters to you provides the resilience and determination needed to overcome obstacles.

A practical way to ensure your goals align with your values is to integrate them into your daily decisions and habits. Small, consistent actions that reflect your values reinforce their importance and keep you connected to your larger purpose. For example, if kindness is a core value, you might set a goal to perform one act of generosity each day. If health is a priority, you could commit to preparing nutritious meals or taking time for physical activity. These daily practices serve as reminders of your values and build momentum toward larger goals, creating a sense of alignment in both the short and long term.

Living a life where goals are aligned with values creates a sense of harmony and authenticity. It allows you to pursue success on your own terms, rather than chasing achievements that leave you feeling empty or unfulfilled. By grounding your aspirations in what truly matters to you, every step you take becomes an expression of your unique identity and purpose. This alignment not only enhances your personal satisfaction but also strengthens your ability to contribute meaningfully to the world around you. It is through this connection between values and goals that you create a life that feels both intentional and deeply rewarding.

Strategic Planning for Success

Success rarely happens by chance. It is often the result of careful thought, deliberate preparation, and strategic planning. While ambition and hard work are vital, they alone are not enough to guarantee meaningful outcomes. Without a clear structure or plan, even the most determined efforts can become scattered and inefficient. Strategic planning is the process of charting the course toward your objectives, laying out the steps, resources, and priorities required to achieve them. It transforms vague ideas into actionable pathways, ensuring that your energy is directed toward purposeful and sustainable progress.

The first step in strategic planning is defining the destination. You cannot create a map without knowing where you want to go. This requires more than setting vague aspirations or wishful thinking—it demands specificity and focus. For instance, rather than resolving to "become successful," you might aim to build a thriving online business that generates a steady income within two years. The clearer and more precise the goal, the easier it becomes to design a plan that leads to it. Defining your destination also involves understanding what success means to you personally, as it will look different for everyone. What fulfills one individual may not resonate with another, so clarity about your unique vision is essential.

Once the destination is established, the next step is to assess your current position. This requires an honest evaluation of where you stand, including your skills, resources, and limitations. Self-awareness is critical in this stage. For instance, if your goal is to transition into a leadership role, you might recognize that while you excel in technical expertise, you lack experience in managing teams. Identifying gaps like this is not a setback but an opportunity to focus your efforts where they are most needed. Equally important is taking stock of the resources—time, finances, connections, or knowledge—you already have at your disposal. Understanding your starting point provides a realistic foundation for building your plan.

A strategic plan is incomplete without prioritization. Not all tasks or actions carry the same weight, and trying to tackle everything at once leads to burnout and inefficiency. Determining what is most important allows you to allocate your time and resources effectively. One useful approach is to identify the high-impact actions that will bring you closer to your goal. For instance, if your aim is to publish a book, spending time refining your writing and researching the publishing process will likely yield greater results than focusing on less critical tasks like designing a book cover too early in the process. Clear priorities ensure that your efforts are concentrated where they matter most.

Time management is another cornerstone of strategic planning. Even the most well-thought-out plan can falter without careful attention to how time is allocated. Breaking your larger goal into smaller, more manageable deadlines creates a sense of urgency and keeps you accountable. For example, if you're working toward launching a small business, you might set a timeline for completing a business plan within three months, securing funding within six, and launching within a year. These incremental deadlines not only make the process feel less overwhelming but also provide measurable milestones to track your progress. Discipline in adhering to these timelines is critical to maintaining momentum.

Flexibility is an often-overlooked but essential element of strategic planning. While it is important to have a clear roadmap, unexpected challenges and opportunities are inevitable. Rigidly adhering to a plan without adapting to changing circumstances can limit your ability to succeed. For instance, a market shift might require you to pivot your business strategy, or personal circumstances might force you to adjust your timelines. Flexibility does not mean abandoning your goals—it means being willing to revise your approach when necessary. A successful strategic plan is one that evolves alongside you, remaining relevant and responsive to the realities you face.

Accountability plays a vital role in ensuring that a strategic plan is executed effectively. Many people lose momentum because they lack structure or external pressure to follow through. Sharing your plan with someone you trust, such as a mentor, colleague, or friend, can provide the accountability needed to stay on track. Regular check-ins, whether with yourself or someone else, create opportunities to evaluate your progress, celebrate achievements, and recalibrate your efforts if needed. This accountability not only helps you stay focused but also reinforces your commitment to the plan, even when motivation wanes.

A well-crafted strategic plan also requires a long-term perspective. Many goals take time to achieve, and it's easy to become discouraged if immediate results are not visible. Patience and persistence are essential. For example, an entrepreneur might spend months refining a product or service before it gains traction in the market. Without a long-term outlook, the slow pace of progress could lead to frustration and abandonment of the goal. Strategic planning helps counteract this by providing a clear vision of the end result and the steps required to get there. This perspective keeps you grounded, reminding you that meaningful success is often the result of consistent effort over time.

Reflection is a critical yet often neglected aspect of strategic planning. As you work toward your goals, taking time to evaluate your progress and learn from your experiences ensures that you remain on the right path. Reflection allows you to identify what is working, what isn't, and where adjustments are needed. For instance, if you notice that a particular strategy is not yielding the desired results, you can pivot before wasting further time and resources. Regular reflection also provides an opportunity to celebrate your achievements, no matter how small, reinforcing your confidence and motivation.

Strategic planning is not just about reaching a goal; it is about creating a framework for intentional and purposeful action. It ensures that your efforts are aligned with your vision, that your resources are used effectively, and that you remain adaptable in the face of challenges. By taking the time to define your destination, assess your starting point, prioritize actions, and build in flexibility, you create a roadmap that maximizes your chances of success. This process transforms abstract aspirations into concrete achievements, empowering you to pursue your goals with clarity, focus, and confidence. Strategic planning is not merely a tool for success—it is a mindset, a way of approaching life with purpose and determination.

Implementation and Follow through

Ideas and plans, no matter how meticulously crafted, remain inert without action. Implementation is the bridge between intention and reality, the process of transforming concepts into tangible outcomes. While it is easy to become enamored with the excitement of planning, the true test lies in execution. This is where the abstract meets the practical, where obstacles arise, and where persistence becomes a critical factor. Follow-through is not merely the act of completing tasks; it is a sustained commitment to seeing a goal through to its conclusion, regardless of setbacks or distractions. Together, implementation and follow-through form the backbone of achievement, ensuring that aspirations evolve into accomplishments.

The first step in implementation is taking decisive action. Even the most elaborate plans can falter if they remain confined to the realm of ideas. Action creates momentum, and momentum fuels progress. Often, the hardest part is simply starting. The initial steps may feel uncertain or clumsy, but they are essential in breaking inertia. Consider someone launching a small business. They might spend months refining their business plan, researching markets, and brainstorming strategies, but until they take that first concrete step—whether it's filing for a business license, securing funding, or reaching out to potential clients—their dream remains hypothetical. Action transforms potential into progress, setting the stage for further development.

Clarity is crucial during the implementation phase. Without a clear sense of what needs to be done, it is easy to become overwhelmed or distracted. Breaking a larger goal into smaller, actionable steps provides a roadmap for progress. For instance, if your objective is to write a novel, focusing on writing one chapter at a time or setting daily word count targets makes the task more manageable. Each completed step serves as a building block, gradually constructing the larger outcome. This approach not only simplifies the process but also provides a sense of accomplishment along the way, reinforcing your motivation to continue.

Discipline is the engine that drives follow-through. Enthusiasm can wane, distractions can arise, and challenges can test your resolve, but discipline keeps you moving forward. It is not about relying on fleeting bursts of motivation but about cultivating habits and routines that prioritize consistent effort. For example, an athlete training for a marathon may not feel inspired to run every day, but their commitment to a structured training schedule ensures they stay on track. Discipline requires setting boundaries, saying no to distractions, and dedicating the necessary time and energy to your goals, even when it feels inconvenient or difficult. It is this consistency that separates those who achieve their aspirations from those who merely dream.

Accountability plays a pivotal role in ensuring follow-through. When you hold yourself accountable—or enlist the support of others to do so—you create a layer of responsibility that reinforces your commitment. Sharing your goals with a trusted friend, mentor, or colleague provides an external source of encouragement and pressure. They can offer feedback, celebrate your progress, and remind you of your intentions when your resolve begins to waver. For instance, someone training for a fitness goal might find it helpful to work with a personal trainer or join a group class where others help keep them on track. Accountability fosters a sense of obligation, not in a burdensome way, but as a tool to sustain focus and effort.

Flexibility is an often-underestimated aspect of successful implementation. While it is essential to stay committed to your goals, rigidity can be counterproductive when faced with unforeseen challenges or changes in circumstances. Life is unpredictable, and plans often require adjustment. For example, a project manager working on a tight deadline might encounter unexpected delays from suppliers, necessitating a shift in timelines or strategies. Flexibility allows you to adapt without losing sight of the ultimate objective. It is about responding to challenges creatively and finding alternative paths forward, rather than abandoning the goal altogether. This adaptability ensures that obstacles become temporary detours rather than insurmountable roadblocks.

Measuring progress is a critical component of follow-through. Without regular evaluation, it is difficult to know whether your efforts are yielding results or if adjustments are needed. Setting measurable milestones and tracking your achievements provides a clear picture of where you stand. For instance, a student preparing for an exam might set weekly study goals and periodically test themselves to gauge their understanding. This feedback loop not only helps identify areas for improvement but also reinforces the sense of advancement, boosting confidence and motivation. Celebrating these milestones, no matter how small, creates positive reinforcement that sustains momentum.

One of the most significant barriers to implementation is fear—fear of failure, fear of imperfection, or even fear of success. These fears can manifest as procrastination or self-doubt, paralyzing progress before it even begins. Overcoming this requires a shift in mindset. Rather than viewing setbacks as failures, see them as opportunities to learn and grow. Embrace the idea that progress is rarely linear and that mistakes are an inherent part of the process. For example, an entrepreneur might launch a product that initially underperforms, but by analyzing feedback and making adjustments, they refine their offering and ultimately achieve greater success. The willingness to act in the face of uncertainty is what separates those who achieve their goals from those who remain trapped by hesitation.

Sustaining follow-through often involves reconnecting with your initial motivation. It is easy to lose sight of the bigger picture when caught up in the day-to-day grind of implementation. Taking time to reflect on why you started and the impact your goal will have can reignite your passion and drive. For instance, a nonprofit leader working on a challenging fundraising campaign might revisit the stories of those they aim to help, reminding themselves of the purpose behind their efforts. This renewed sense of purpose provides the emotional fuel needed to push through periods of doubt or fatigue.

Measuring Progress and Adjusting Course

Progress is rarely a straight line. The path to achieving any goal is often marked by unexpected challenges, periods of stagnation, and moments of triumph. To navigate this journey successfully, it is crucial to understand where you stand at any given point and how far you've come. Measuring progress provides clarity, a sense of accomplishment, and the ability to evaluate whether your current strategies are effective. Equally important is the willingness to adjust course when necessary, ensuring that your efforts remain aligned with your ultimate objective. Together, these practices form the foundation for sustained growth and purposeful action.

A clear system for measuring progress begins with defining measurable benchmarks. These benchmarks serve as tangible indicators of advancement, allowing you to track how close you are to your goal. For example, if your goal is to save a specific amount of money by the end of the year, tracking your savings monthly gives you a clear picture of your progress. Similarly, if you are training for a marathon, recording your running distances and times on a weekly basis allows you to see improvement over time. These metrics create a sense of structure, transforming an abstract goal into manageable and observable milestones.

Measuring progress is not just about numbers or data; it's also about reflecting on qualitative aspects. Personal growth, skill development, and emotional resilience are often harder to quantify but are just as important. For instance, someone pursuing a creative goal, such as learning to paint, might not measure progress solely by the number of completed artworks but also by their increased confidence, improved technique, or the joy they experience while creating. Taking time to reflect on these intangible aspects enriches your understanding of your journey, reminding you that progress is multi-dimensional.

Regular evaluation is essential to ensure that your efforts are moving you closer to your goal. This involves setting aside time to review your progress, identify patterns, and assess whether your current strategies are effective. For instance, an entrepreneur working to grow their business might analyze monthly sales data, customer feedback, and marketing performance to determine what's working and what isn't. This process of evaluation not only highlights successes but also reveals areas for improvement or adjustment. Without regular check-ins, it's easy to lose sight of the bigger picture or waste time on approaches that yield little return.

While measuring progress is vital, it's equally important to recognize the potential for setbacks and plateaus. Progress is rarely linear, and expecting constant forward motion can lead to frustration or disillusionment. Plateaus, in particular, are a natural part of any growth process. For example, someone learning a new language might experience rapid improvement in the early stages but then feel as though their progress has slowed. This doesn't mean they're failing; it simply reflects the complexity of mastering a skill. Recognizing the inevitability of plateaus allows you to approach them with patience and persistence, rather than viewing them as insurmountable obstacles.

Adjusting course is a natural and necessary response to the insights gained from measuring progress. If something isn't working, sticking rigidly to the same approach will only lead to frustration and wasted effort. Flexibility allows you to pivot, refine your strategies, or even redefine your goal if circumstances change. For instance, a student preparing for an exam might realize that their initial study method isn't effective and decide to adopt a different approach, such as joining a study group or seeking additional resources. These adjustments are not signs of failure but of adaptability and resilience. They demonstrate a commitment to the goal and a willingness to learn from experience.

Sometimes, adjusting course requires revisiting the goal itself. Life is dynamic, and what seemed important or achievable at one point may no longer align with your priorities or circumstances. For example, an individual aiming to climb the corporate ladder might discover over time that their values have shifted, and they now prioritize work-life balance over career advancement. In such cases, it's important to reevaluate the goal and ensure it still reflects your authentic aspirations. Letting go of a goal that no longer serves you is not a failure; it's an act of self-awareness and growth.

Celebrating milestones along the way is a crucial aspect of measuring progress. These moments of recognition provide motivation, reinforce positive behavior, and remind you of how far you've come. For instance, a writer completing the first draft of their manuscript might celebrate by sharing the achievement with friends or taking a well-deserved break. These celebrations don't have to be extravagant; even small gestures can have a powerful impact on your mindset. By acknowledging your progress, you cultivate a sense of gratitude and pride that fuels further effort.

Measuring progress also fosters accountability. When you have a clear record of your achievements and setbacks, it becomes easier to stay honest with yourself about whether you're putting in the necessary effort. Sharing your progress with others can further enhance this accountability. For example, someone working on a fitness goal might regularly update a friend or coach on their performance, creating an external layer of responsibility. This shared accountability not only keeps you on track but also provides encouragement and support during challenging times.

Perhaps one of the most important aspects of measuring progress and adjusting course is maintaining a growth mindset. Viewing challenges as opportunities to learn rather than as failures allows you to stay resilient and adaptable. For example, an artist whose work faces criticism might use the feedback to improve their craft, rather than becoming discouraged. This mindset fosters a sense of curiosity and openness, encouraging you to embrace the process of growth rather than fixating solely on the end result.

Chapter 6: Living with Purpose

Discovering Your Life Mission

A life mission is more than a lofty ideal or a fleeting ambition; it is the essence of what gives your existence purpose and direction. It is the compass that guides your decisions, the foundation upon which your values rest, and the thread that weaves meaning into your daily life. Discovering your life mission is not about finding a definitive answer overnight. It is a process of introspection, exploration, and sometimes trial and error. It requires peeling back the layers of societal expectations, personal insecurities, and external pressures to uncover what truly resonates with your core identity. When you align your actions with your life mission, you create a sense of harmony and fulfillment that extends far beyond individual achievements.

Understanding your life mission begins with reflection. Often, the clues to discovering it lie in the patterns of your past. Think back to the moments when you felt most alive, connected, or at peace. These moments often hold subtle indicators of what matters most to you. For instance, consider the teacher who feels a spark of joy when a struggling student grasps a difficult concept. This experience might point to a deeper calling to nurture and empower others. Similarly, someone who has always been drawn to the beauty of nature might find their mission tied to environmental conservation. These moments, though small, are windows into what fulfills you on a profound level.

Your passions and talents are also critical pieces of the puzzle. A life mission is often found at the intersection of what you love and what you're naturally inclined to do well. Take a moment to consider the activities or causes that consistently draw your attention. What do you do that feels effortless yet deeply rewarding? For some, this might be a creative pursuit like painting or writing. For others, it could be problem-solving, mentoring, or building connections. These passions and talents are not random—they are unique gifts that point to how you can make a meaningful contribution to the world.

However, a life mission is not solely about personal fulfillment. It also involves understanding how your unique abilities can serve others. The most enduring missions are those that create value beyond yourself, whether by improving lives, fostering understanding, or contributing to a greater cause. For example, an entrepreneur might discover their mission in creating products that solve real-world problems, while a caregiver might find meaning in helping others navigate difficult times with dignity and compassion. Serving others does not mean sacrificing your happiness—it means finding a purpose that intertwines your joy with the well-being of those around you.

Fear and doubt can often obscure the path to discovering your life mission. You may question whether you are capable of making a meaningful impact or whether your aspirations are realistic. These doubts are natural, but they should not deter you from exploring what truly matters to you. Start by silencing the external noise—the voices of societal expectations, familial pressures, or comparisons to others—and instead focus inward. What would you pursue if there were no limitations, no fear of judgment, and no constraints? The answer to this question often provides a glimpse of what your life mission might entail.

Sometimes, your mission emerges from challenges or adversities you've faced. Difficult experiences, while painful, often shape your perspective and grant you unique insights. Consider someone who has overcome a significant health challenge. They might feel called to advocate for others in similar situations or work to improve healthcare systems. Adversity can ignite a passion for change, turning personal struggles into a source of strength and purpose. Your mission does not have to erase the hardships you've endured, but it can transform them into a driving force for something greater.

The process of discovering your life mission is not static; it evolves as you grow and gain new experiences. What feels meaningful at one stage of life may shift as your priorities, values, and circumstances change. For example, a young professional may initially find purpose in career advancement, only to later realize that their mission lies in fostering a family or contributing to their community. This evolution is not a sign of inconsistency but of growth. Embrace these changes as opportunities to refine and deepen your understanding of what truly drives you.

Connection with others can also illuminate your life mission. The people you admire or feel inspired by often embody qualities or pursuits that resonate with you. Surrounding yourself with individuals who challenge, support, and encourage you can help clarify your path. Conversations with mentors, loved ones, or even strangers can provide fresh perspectives and insights that you might not have considered on your own. These interactions are not about finding someone else's mission to adopt, but about uncovering your own through shared experiences and reflections.

It is important to recognize that your life mission does not have to be grandiose or world-changing to be meaningful. While some may dedicate their lives to solving global issues or leading large-scale movements, others might find their purpose in quieter, more personal ways. A parent nurturing their children, a friend offering unwavering support, or a craftsman dedicating themselves to their art—all of these paths can hold profound meaning. Your mission is unique to you, and its significance lies not in its scale but in the authenticity with which you live it.

Taking steps toward your life mission requires courage and commitment. It may involve taking risks, stepping into the unknown, or making sacrifices. However, the rewards—fulfillment, clarity, and a sense of direction—far outweigh the challenges. Living in alignment with your mission allows you to approach each day with intention and purpose, knowing that your actions reflect who you truly are. It is not about perfection or achieving a specific endpoint; it is about the ongoing journey of living in a way that feels true to your essence.

Discovering your life mission is one of the most profound journeys you can undertake. It is not a destination to be reached but a process of continuous exploration and growth. By reflecting on your passions, talents, experiences, and the impact you wish to have on others, you uncover the purpose that gives your life depth and meaning. This mission, once recognized, becomes a guiding force, shaping your choices and actions in ways that bring fulfillment not only to yourself but to those whose lives you touch.

Creating a Personal Vision

A personal vision is the cornerstone of a purposeful life, serving as a vivid picture of the future you want to create for yourself. It goes beyond short-term goals or fleeting desires, reaching deep into the essence of who you are and what you truly value. A personal vision provides clarity, focus, and motivation, acting as a guiding light when life presents uncertainty or competing priorities. It is not a rigid plan but a dynamic and evolving framework that helps you align your daily actions with your long-term aspirations. Crafting this vision is both an introspective journey and a practical exercise, requiring honesty, imagination, and deliberate thought.

The process of creating a personal vision begins with self-awareness. To envision the life you want, you first need to understand who you are. This involves reflecting on your core values, the principles that define your character and shape your decisions. Values are not borrowed from others or dictated by society; they are deeply personal and unique to you.

For example, one person might prioritize creativity and freedom, while another values family and stability. Identifying these guiding principles can provide a foundation for your vision, ensuring that it reflects what genuinely matters to you rather than external expectations.

Equally important is examining your passions—the activities, causes, or pursuits that ignite your enthusiasm and bring you joy. Passions are often an indication of what gives your life meaning. They may be tied to your natural talents, but they don't have to be. For instance, someone who loves storytelling might envision a future as an author or filmmaker, while another person who feels deeply connected to the environment might dream of working in conservation. Your passions do not need to fit neatly into a career or traditional framework; they simply serve as clues to what fulfills you on a deeper level.

Once you've gained clarity on your values and passions, it's time to think about your long-term aspirations. What kind of legacy do you want to leave behind? How do you want to impact the people around you or the world at large? These questions prompt you to consider not just what you want to achieve but who you want to become. For example, someone might aspire to create a thriving business, not solely for financial success, but to foster innovation or provide opportunities for others. Another person might envision a life filled with meaningful relationships, personal growth, and contributions to their community. These aspirations help define the overarching purpose of your vision.

Imagination plays a crucial role in this process. Allow yourself to dream without limitations, setting aside practical concerns or fears of failure temporarily. Picture your ideal life in vivid detail: Where are you? What are you doing? Who is with you? How do you feel? Engage all your senses to create a rich and compelling mental image of the future you desire. For instance, if you dream of living in a coastal town while running your own business, imagine the sound of the waves, the smell of the sea air, and the satisfaction of working on projects that excite you. This exercise not only makes your vision more tangible but also fuels your motivation to pursue it.

While dreaming big is essential, grounding your vision in reality is equally important. Consider the resources, skills, and opportunities you currently have, as well as the challenges you might face. This doesn't mean limiting your ambitions but rather creating a roadmap that bridges the gap between where you are and where you want to be. For example, if your vision involves switching careers, you might need to acquire new qualifications, build a network in your desired field, or save money to support the transition. By acknowledging these practicalities, you set yourself up for success while maintaining the integrity of your vision.

A personal vision is not static; it evolves as you grow and your circumstances change. Life is unpredictable, and the goals that resonate with you now may shift over time. This flexibility is not a sign of inconsistency but a reflection of your adaptability and self-awareness. For instance, someone who once dreamed of climbing the corporate ladder might later find fulfillment in starting a nonprofit or prioritizing their family life. Revisiting and refining your vision periodically ensures that it remains aligned with your current values and aspirations, allowing it to continue serving as a source of inspiration and direction.

Articulating your vision in writing can make it more powerful and concrete. A written vision statement captures the essence of what you want to achieve and serves as a reminder of your purpose. It doesn't need to be lengthy or perfect; it simply needs to resonate with you. For example, a vision statement might read, "I will create a life where I wake up excited to contribute to meaningful projects, surrounded by people I love, while maintaining balance and creativity in everything I do." This statement becomes a touchstone, helping you stay focused when distractions or doubts arise.

Living in alignment with your personal vision requires consistent action. Each decision you make, no matter how small, can either bring you closer to or further from the life you want to create. For instance, if your vision includes financial independence, the choice to save money rather than spend impulsively is a step toward that goal. Over time, these small, deliberate actions compound, turning your vision into reality. It's important to celebrate progress along the way, acknowledging the milestones you've reached and the growth you've experienced.

A personal vision is not just a tool for achieving goals; it is a reflection of who you are and what you stand for. It provides clarity in moments of doubt, motivation during challenges, and a sense of purpose that transcends daily routines. By taking the time to craft a vision that is authentic and meaningful, you create a life that feels intentional and fulfilling. This vision becomes the lens through which you view opportunities and make decisions, ensuring that your actions are always aligned with the future you want to create.

Living Authentically

Authenticity is the quiet power that transforms a life from ordinary to extraordinary. To live authentically means to align your actions, choices, and relationships with your true self, without pretense or fear of judgment. It is not about perfection or living without flaws, but about embracing the uniqueness of who you are and carrying that truth into every aspect of your life. Authenticity is the foundation of a meaningful existence, yet it is often obscured by societal expectations, external pressures, and the fear of vulnerability. The journey to living authentically is not always straightforward, but it is profoundly liberating.

At its core, authenticity begins with self-awareness. To live as your true self, you must first understand who that self is. This requires a deep and honest exploration of your values, beliefs, and desires. What do you stand for? What drives you? What brings you joy, fulfillment, or peace? These questions are not always easy to answer, especially when you've spent years molding yourself to fit the expectations of others. For example, someone who has pursued a particular career path because it was expected of them might need to step back and ask whether that choice truly aligns with their passions and values. Self-awareness is about peeling away the layers of conditioning and reconnecting with the essence of who you are.

Authenticity also demands courage. Living authentically often means stepping away from the safety of conformity and risking disapproval or misunderstanding. It requires you to show up in the world as you are, even when doing so feels uncomfortable or exposes you to criticism. For instance, an artist who creates unconventional work may face skepticism or rejection but chooses to stay true to their vision rather than compromising for acceptance. This courage is not about being fearless—it is about moving forward despite fear, trusting that the rewards of living authentically outweigh the risks.

Vulnerability is a key element of authenticity. To be authentic is to allow others to see you, flaws and all, without hiding behind masks or façades. This can be especially challenging in a world that often equates vulnerability with weakness. However, vulnerability is, in fact, a profound strength. It fosters genuine connections, invites trust, and allows you to experience relationships and interactions on a deeper level. For example, sharing your struggles or fears with a close friend might feel uncomfortable, but it can also strengthen your bond and provide the support you need. Vulnerability is the bridge between who you are and how you relate to others, making it an essential part of living authentically.

Living authentically also means aligning your actions with your values. It's one thing to know what you stand for, but another to let those principles guide your decisions and behaviors. Authenticity requires consistency between what you believe and how you live. For example, someone who values environmental sustainability might make choices that reflect that commitment, such as reducing waste or supporting eco-friendly businesses. This alignment creates a sense of integrity and self-respect, as you know that your actions are a true reflection of your inner self. It also inspires trust and respect from others, as people are naturally drawn to those who live with conviction.

One of the most significant barriers to authenticity is the fear of judgment. The desire to be liked or accepted can lead to behaviors that contradict your true self, as you prioritize others' opinions over your own truth. This fear is deeply ingrained, often stemming from early experiences where approval was tied to conformity. Overcoming it requires a shift in perspective. Rather than seeking validation from others, focus on cultivating self-acceptance. Recognize that not everyone will understand or agree with your choices, and that's okay. Authenticity is not about pleasing everyone—it's about living in a way that is true to yourself.

Boundaries are another essential aspect of living authentically. When you lack boundaries, you risk compromising your values, needs, or well-being to accommodate others. Setting boundaries is not about being selfish; it's about honoring your own needs while respecting those of others. For example, if you value your time and energy, you might choose to say no to commitments that don't align with your priorities. Boundaries create space for you to live authentically, without being pulled in directions that detract from your sense of self.

Authenticity is not a destination but a lifelong practice. As you grow and evolve, your understanding of yourself will deepen, and your expression of authenticity may change. This is not a contradiction—it is a natural part of being human. For instance, someone who once identified strongly with a particular career or lifestyle may find that their values shift over time, leading them to pursue a different path. Living authentically means embracing this evolution and allowing your life to reflect your current truth, rather than clinging to outdated identities or expectations.

The rewards of living authentically are profound. When you align with your true self, you experience a sense of freedom and peace that cannot be achieved through external validation. Your relationships become more meaningful, as they are built on genuine connection rather than pretense. You find greater fulfillment in your choices, knowing that they reflect who you truly are. Even challenges and setbacks take on a different quality, as you face them with the confidence that comes from living in alignment with your values.

Living authentically is not always easy, but it is always worth it. It requires self-awareness, courage, and a commitment to honoring your truth, even in the face of challenges. It is a journey of peeling back layers, embracing vulnerability, and aligning your actions with your values. By choosing authenticity, you create a life that is not only fulfilling but uniquely your own. It is a way of being that honors both who you are and the world you wish to create, offering a sense of purpose and connection that enriches every aspect of your existence.

Chapter 7: Sustaining Personal Growth

Building Sustainable Habits

Habits shape the foundation of our daily lives, quietly steering the direction of our choices, productivity, and overall well-being. They are the small, repeated actions that form the framework of who we are and who we are becoming. While habits have the power to propel us toward success and fulfillment, they can just as easily hold us back if they fail to align with our values or goals. The key to transformation lies not in grand gestures or fleeting resolutions but in building sustainable habits—practices that integrate seamlessly into your life and stand the test of time. This process requires intention, patience, and a deep understanding of how habits are formed and maintained.

The process begins with clarity. To build habits that last, you must first identify what truly matters to you. It is not enough to adopt a habit simply because it seems trendy or because someone else swears by it. Sustainable habits are rooted in your personal goals, values, and aspirations. For example, if you aim to improve your physical health, a habit like daily exercise or mindful eating becomes meaningful because it aligns with your vision of a healthier, more vibrant life. Clarity ensures that your habits are not arbitrary but purposeful, providing motivation even when the initial excitement fades.

Small, incremental changes are the cornerstone of sustainable habit formation. It's tempting to overhaul your life overnight, but drastic changes are rarely sustainable. Instead, focusing on small, manageable steps ensures that you can incorporate new habits without overwhelming yourself. For instance, if you aspire to read more, starting with a goal of reading just five pages a day is far more attainable than committing to finishing a book every week. These small actions may seem insignificant at first, but their cumulative impact over time is profound. They allow you to build momentum gradually, transforming what once felt like effort into second nature.

Consistency is the bedrock of any habit. The brain thrives on repetition, as it allows new behaviors to become ingrained over time. However, consistency does not mean perfection. Life is unpredictable, and there will inevitably be days when you miss the mark. What matters is your ability to return to the habit without guilt or self-criticism. For example, if you miss a workout, it's easy to let that lapse snowball into a week or month of inactivity. Instead, approaching the situation with self-compassion and resuming the habit the next day ensures that one misstep doesn't derail your progress. Sustainable habits are not about a flawless streak but about resilience in the face of setbacks.

The environment you create plays a significant role in supporting or hindering your habits. Human behavior is heavily influenced by surroundings, often more than we realize. Adjusting your environment to make positive habits easier and undesirable ones more difficult can dramatically increase your chances of success. For example, if you want to eat healthier, keeping fresh fruits and vegetables readily available while removing junk food from your home creates an environment that supports your goal. Similarly, if you want to spend less time on your phone, placing it in another room while you work reduces the temptation to check it mindlessly. By shaping your environment, you reduce reliance on willpower and make the path to sustaining new habits smoother.

Accountability can be a powerful tool in habit formation. Sharing your intentions with someone you trust, whether a friend, family member, or mentor, creates an external layer of responsibility. For instance, deciding to meet a workout partner at the gym makes it less likely that you'll skip the session. Accountability doesn't have to involve another person; even tracking your progress in a journal or app can serve as a form of self-accountability. Seeing tangible evidence of your efforts reinforces your commitment and provides a sense of accomplishment, which motivates you to keep going.

Reward systems can also enhance the sustainability of habits. Positive reinforcement strengthens the association between the habit and a sense of satisfaction. However, rewards don't have to be elaborate or materialistic. Often, the intrinsic satisfaction of progress is enough. For example, the endorphin boost after a run or the sense of clarity after meditating can serve as natural rewards that reinforce the behavior. Over time, the habit itself becomes the reward, as it integrates into your identity and contributes to your overall well-being.

Sustainable habits require adaptability. Life is not static, and circumstances change. A habit that worked well in one phase of your life may no longer be practical or relevant. For instance, a morning workout routine might be ideal when you have a flexible schedule but challenging during a period of increased responsibilities. Rather than abandoning the habit altogether, adapting it to fit your current reality ensures that you remain consistent in some form. This flexibility prevents the all-or-nothing mindset that often leads to abandoning habits entirely when perfection isn't possible.

Understanding the "why" behind your habits adds depth and meaning to your efforts. It's easy to lose motivation when a habit feels like a chore or obligation, but connecting it to a larger purpose keeps you engaged. For instance, rather than viewing exercise as a means to an end, such as weight loss, reframing it as a way to feel stronger, more energized, or mentally clear shifts your perspective. This intrinsic motivation makes the habit feel less like a task and more like an investment in your overall well-being.

Over time, sustainable habits become part of your identity. They transition from being something you do to being an integral part of who you are. For example, someone who consistently writes every day begins to see themselves as a writer, while someone who prioritizes healthy eating starts to identify as someone who values nourishment and self-care. This shift in identity reinforces the habit, as it becomes intertwined with your sense of self. When a habit aligns with your identity, it no longer feels like an obligation but a natural extension of your values and priorities.

Building sustainable habits is not about perfection or quick fixes. It is about creating a foundation of intentional practices that support the life you want to live. By starting small, remaining consistent, and adapting to life's changes, you cultivate habits that endure. These habits, rooted in purpose and aligned with your values, become the building blocks of a meaningful and fulfilling life. They are not just actions you perform but expressions of who you are, shaping your future one small step at a time.

Maintaining Long term Motivation

Motivation is often seen as a fleeting force, something that surges in moments of inspiration but gradually fades over time. Yet the ability to maintain motivation over the long term is what distinguishes those who persevere from those who abandon their goals midway. It is not a matter of willpower alone, but a deliberate practice of nurturing the drive that fuels your actions. Long-term motivation stems from a combination of clarity, adaptability, and resilience, all of which work together to create sustained energy and focus. Understanding how to cultivate this enduring force can transform the way you approach challenges and aspirations.

At the heart of lasting motivation is a clear sense of purpose. When you know exactly why you are working toward a goal, it becomes easier to stay committed, even when progress feels slow or obstacles arise.

Purpose serves as a compass, guiding you through moments of doubt and reminding you of the larger picture. Consider an athlete training for a marathon. The early mornings, grueling runs, and physical discomfort are all made bearable by the vision of crossing the finish line. Similarly, when your actions align with a goal that holds deep meaning for you, the effort required feels worthwhile. Without a clear "why," motivation becomes fragile, easily shaken by setbacks or distractions.

Breaking larger goals into smaller, manageable milestones is another essential strategy for sustaining motivation. A daunting, far-off objective can feel overwhelming, making it difficult to maintain momentum. However, when the journey is divided into achievable steps, each small success becomes a source of encouragement. For example, someone saving for a major purchase might feel disheartened by the total amount needed, but reaching smaller savings targets along the way provides a sense of progress and accomplishment. These incremental victories reinforce your belief in your ability to succeed and keep you engaged with the process.

Routine and consistency play a significant role in maintaining long-term motivation. When you integrate actions toward your goal into your daily or weekly schedule, they become habits rather than sporadic efforts. This consistency reduces reliance on fleeting bursts of inspiration, allowing progress to continue even when motivation wanes. For instance, a writer who commits to drafting a certain number of words each day is far more likely to complete a book than someone who writes only when they feel inspired. By embedding your efforts into a routine, you create a structure that supports sustained action.

Adaptability is equally important. Life rarely unfolds exactly as planned, and rigid adherence to a specific path can lead to frustration or burnout. Maintaining motivation requires the flexibility to adjust your approach when circumstances change. For instance, someone pursuing a fitness goal might encounter an injury that prevents them from following their original workout plan. Rather than giving up entirely, they could explore alternative exercises or focus on nutrition until they recover. This ability to pivot keeps momentum alive, ensuring that temporary setbacks don't derail long-term progress.

One of the most overlooked aspects of motivation is the role of self-compassion. It is easy to be hard on yourself when you fall short of your expectations, but excessive self-criticism can erode motivation over time. Instead, treating yourself with understanding and kindness when challenges arise allows you to bounce back more quickly. For example, if you miss a deadline or make a mistake, acknowledging that setbacks are a natural part of any journey can help you refocus without the burden of guilt. Self-compassion fosters resilience, which is essential for sustaining motivation through difficulties.

The people you surround yourself with also have a profound impact on your ability to stay motivated. Positive, supportive relationships can inspire and encourage you, while negative influences can drain your energy and confidence. For instance, sharing your goals with someone who believes in your potential can provide accountability and reinforcement, while spending time with those who dismiss or undermine your efforts can make it harder to stay committed. Cultivating a network of individuals who share your values or aspirations creates an environment that nurtures your motivation and helps you stay focused.

Celebrating progress is another powerful way to sustain your drive. It's tempting to wait until you've achieved the ultimate goal to acknowledge your efforts, but recognizing smaller milestones along the way is equally important. These celebrations don't have to be elaborate; even a simple acknowledgment of your progress can have a significant impact on your mindset. For example, treating yourself to a favorite meal after completing a challenging project or taking time to reflect on how far you've come can reinforce the sense of accomplishment that keeps motivation alive.

While external rewards and recognition can provide short-term boosts, intrinsic motivation is what truly sustains you over time. This comes from the enjoyment or fulfillment you derive from the process itself, rather than from external validation. For instance, a musician who practices not just to perform but because they genuinely love creating music is more likely to stay motivated in the long run. Finding ways to connect with the intrinsic value of your efforts—whether it's the sense of growth, mastery, or contribution they bring—ensures that your motivation remains rooted in something enduring.

Continuous Learning and Adaptation

Growth is an intrinsic part of life, and at the heart of growth lies the ability to continuously learn and adapt. Life's challenges, opportunities, and uncertainties demand more than static knowledge or rigid thinking—they require an openness to evolve and a willingness to embrace change. Continuous learning and adaptation are not merely about acquiring new skills or information; they are about cultivating a mindset that thrives on curiosity, resilience, and the pursuit of understanding. This dynamic process ensures that you remain relevant, capable, and fulfilled, no matter what paths your life takes.

Curiosity serves as the foundation for lifelong learning. It is the natural desire to explore, question, and understand the world. This innate drive often begins in childhood, when the simplest things—how a bird flies or why the sky changes colors—spark endless questions. Unfortunately, as people grow older, curiosity can become stifled by routine, fear of failure, or the assumption that they already know enough. Reawakening this sense of wonder is essential. Whether it's delving into a new subject, experimenting with a creative pursuit, or seeking to understand a differing perspective, curiosity acts as the ignition for learning. For instance, a professional who chooses to explore an unfamiliar industry not only broadens their horizons but often discovers insights that can be applied to their existing expertise. Curiosity keeps knowledge from becoming stagnant; it ensures that learning remains an active and engaging process.

Adaptation, on the other hand, is the ability to respond effectively to change. In a world that evolves rapidly—technologically, socially, and environmentally—adaptability is the skill that allows you to navigate uncertainty. It is not about abandoning your principles or constantly changing direction without purpose; rather, it's about finding ways to adjust your methods while staying true to your goals. Consider someone who loses their job unexpectedly. While the initial shock may be overwhelming, adaptability allows them to reassess their skills, explore new career paths, and ultimately find opportunities they might never have considered otherwise. This flexibility requires both emotional resilience and creative thinking, as it often involves stepping outside your comfort zone and confronting unfamiliar challenges.

Learning is most effective when it is intentional. It's easy to passively absorb information without ever applying it or integrating it into your life. However, deliberate learning—where you actively seek out knowledge with a specific purpose or goal—has a far greater impact. For example, a musician might choose to study an unfamiliar genre not just out of interest, but to enhance their own compositions. Similarly, someone pursuing personal growth might read books, attend workshops, or engage in discussions that challenge their existing beliefs. This intentionality ensures that the time and energy spent learning yield meaningful results, rather than being scattered or superficial.

Failure is an inevitable part of both learning and adaptation. It is through mistakes that some of the most profound lessons emerge. Yet, failure is often viewed with fear or shame, preventing people from taking risks or trying new things. Reframing failure as an opportunity for growth transforms it from a setback into a stepping stone. Consider an entrepreneur whose first business venture fails. While the experience might be disheartening, it also provides invaluable insights into what didn't work, paving the way for a more informed and strategic approach in the future. Embracing failure as a natural and necessary aspect of progress fosters resilience and encourages you to keep moving forward, no matter how many times you stumble.

The practice of reflection enhances both learning and adaptation. Taking time to evaluate your experiences, identify lessons, and recognize patterns allows you to learn more deeply and adapt more effectively. For instance, after completing a major project, reflecting on what went well and what could have been improved equips you with knowledge that can be applied to future endeavors. Reflection is not about dwelling on the past, but about using it as a resource for growth. It helps you connect the dots between where you've been and where you're going, ensuring that each step forward is informed by the wisdom gained along the way.

Community and collaboration amplify the benefits of continuous learning. Engaging with others—whether through mentorship, discussion, or shared experiences—provides perspectives and insights that you might not discover on your own. For example, a writer participating in a critique group gains not only feedback on their work but also exposure to different styles, ideas, and approaches. Learning within a community fosters creativity and innovation, as the exchange of knowledge and experiences inspires new ways of thinking. Collaboration also reinforces the idea that learning is not a solitary journey, but a collective one, enriched by the contributions of others.

Adaptation often requires letting go of what no longer serves you. Clinging to outdated habits, beliefs, or methods can hinder progress and make change more difficult than it needs to be. For example, someone who insists on using traditional marketing techniques in a digital age may struggle to reach their audience effectively. Letting go doesn't mean dismissing the past; it means recognizing when it's time to evolve. This act of release creates space for new opportunities and approaches, ensuring that you remain relevant and effective in an ever-changing world.

The Journey of Self Mastery

Self-mastery is the art of understanding, controlling, and ultimately transcending the limitations of your own mind and behaviors to achieve a state of alignment with your highest potential. It is not confined to a single achievement or moment but is instead a lifelong journey, a process of evolution that demands both discipline and self-awareness. This path is not about perfection, but about progress— about learning to better navigate the intricate relationship between your emotions, thoughts, and actions. The journey is deeply personal, yet its impact extends far beyond the individual, influencing relationships, goals, and the way one interacts with the world.

The foundation of self-mastery lies in self-awareness. Without a clear understanding of who you are, what drives you, and where your strengths and weaknesses lie, growth is impossible. Developing self-awareness requires a willingness to look inward, even when what you find is uncomfortable or challenging. It means observing your thoughts without judgment, recognizing patterns in your behavior, and acknowledging how your choices impact your life and the lives of those around you. For instance, someone prone to anger might notice how their reactions escalate conflicts, turning minor disagreements into larger issues. By becoming aware of these tendencies, they gain the ability to pause, reflect, and choose a more constructive response. Self-awareness is not about criticizing yourself but about seeing yourself clearly enough to take ownership of your growth.

Emotional regulation is a critical component of self-mastery. Emotions are powerful and often unpredictable, capable of clouding judgment and dictating actions in ways that may not align with your long-term goals. Mastering your emotions does not mean suppressing them or pretending they don't exist. Rather, it involves recognizing and understanding them, so you can respond thoughtfully rather than react impulsively. For example, fear might deter someone from taking a necessary risk, but by examining the root of the fear and reframing it as an opportunity for growth, they can move forward despite their apprehension. Emotional regulation empowers you to act in alignment with your values and intentions, even when faced with challenging or high-stakes situations.

Habits play a significant role in the journey of self-mastery. Much of what you do on a daily basis is governed by routines—automatic behaviors that shape your life in profound ways. To achieve mastery over yourself, you must take control of these habits, replacing those that hinder your progress with ones that support your goals. This requires both discipline and patience, as habits are not easily changed overnight. Consider someone striving to improve their physical health. By consistently choosing nutritious foods, exercising regularly, and prioritizing sleep, they gradually transform their daily routines into a lifestyle that supports their well-being. These small, consistent actions compound over time, creating a foundation for sustained growth and achievement.

Self-mastery also involves cultivating a growth mindset. This mindset is characterized by the belief that abilities and intelligence are not fixed traits but can be developed through effort and perseverance. Adopting this perspective shifts your focus from avoiding failure to embracing challenges as opportunities to learn and improve. For instance, an artist who views criticism as a tool for refinement rather than as a personal attack is more likely to grow and evolve in their craft. A growth mindset allows you to approach setbacks with curiosity and resilience, viewing them as integral parts of your journey rather than as obstacles to your success.

Discipline is perhaps one of the most demanding aspects of self-mastery. It requires you to act in accordance with your goals and values, even when motivation is low or distractions are abundant. Discipline is the bridge between intention and action, turning aspirations into realities. For example, a writer working on a novel might feel inspired on some days and uninspired on others, but discipline ensures that they show up to write regardless of how they feel. This consistency builds momentum and reinforces your commitment to your goals, making it easier to persevere over time. Discipline is not about rigid control; it's about making conscious choices that serve your higher purpose.

Another essential aspect of self-mastery is the ability to let go of what no longer serves you. This includes limiting beliefs, toxic relationships, and unproductive habits. Clinging to these elements out of fear or familiarity can keep you trapped in cycles that prevent growth. Letting go is not an easy process—it often involves discomfort and a willingness to confront difficult truths. However, it is also liberating, creating space for new opportunities and perspectives. For example, someone who steps away from a career that no longer aligns with their values may face uncertainty in the short term but ultimately finds greater fulfillment in pursuing work that resonates with their passions.